AF269407

NEHEMIAH
The Wall Builder

Other Biblical Character Studies by Walter C. Kaiser, Jr.

The Lives and Ministries of ELIJAH and ELISHA

ABRAHAM The Friend of God

JOSHUA A True Servant Leader

JOSEPH From Prison to Palace

The Journey from JACOB to Israel

NEHEMIAH The Wall Builder

——✡——

Coming Soon

DAVID A Man After God's Own Heart

MOSES The Man Who Saw the Invisible God

SOLOMON The King with a Listening Heart

THE TWELVE The "Minor" Prophets Speak Today

ZECHARIAH The Quintessence of Old Testament Prophecy

DANIEL The Handwriting is on the Wall

RUTH The Moabite and the Providence of God

ESTHER God Preserves the Jewish Nation

NEHEMIAH
The Wall Builder

Walter C. Kaiser, Jr.

Lederer Books
an imprint of
Messianic Jewish Publishers
Clarksville, MD 21029

Unless otherwise noted, all Scripture quotations are from the *New American Standard Bible*, copyright © 1978 by Thomas Nelson Publishers; the *Complete Jewish Bible*, copyright © 1998 by Messianic Jewish Publishers; or the *New International Version*, copyright © 2002 by the International Bible Society.

Copyright © 2022 by Walter C. Kaiser, Jr. All rights reserved.

Printed in the United States of America

Cover Design by Lisa Rubin,
Messianic Jewish Publishers
Graphic Design by Yvonne Vermillion,
MagicGraphix.com
Editor, George August Koch

1   2022
ISBN 9781951833046

No part of this publication may be reproduced, stored in a retrieval system, or transmitted in any form or by any means without the prior permission of the publisher, except for brief reviews in magazines, or as quotations in another work when full attribution is given.

Published by:
Lederer Books
An imprint of Messianic Jewish Publishers
6120 Day Long Lane
Clarksville, MD 21029

Distributed by:
Messianic Jewish Publishers & Resources
Order line: (800) 410-7367
lederer@messianicjewish.net
www.MessianicJewish.net

DEDICATION

To Robert E. Coleman and, in memoriam of his wife, Marietta,
for their excellence in the ministries of
discipleship and evangelism

Table of Contents

Lesson 1

The Principles and Marks
of a Godly Leader

Nehemiah 1

The opening verse of Nehemiah immediately declares, "Nehemiah, son of Hacaliah." Nehemiah's name means "Jehovah comforts." His father's name means "Jehovah is hidden." Thus, Nehemiah began his own personal account of his memoires as directed by the Holy Spirit.

The first seven chapters of Nehemiah, plus 12:31–13:31, are all written using the first-person pronoun. Thus we get an unusual, unique look into the heart and life of an outstanding servant-leader of God. Nehemiah combined a steady life of prayer and a deep trust in the Lord, along with unusually careful planning, good organizational skills and energetic action in the twelve years of his administration over the province of Judah.

As these memoirs begin, we find that Nehemiah belonged to the group of exiled Jews, who had been carried off as captives to Babylon. But upon returning to Israel from this Babylonian exile, he rose to a high office in the Persian administration. The empire succeeded the earlier Babylonian reign in the Middle East, which came following the Persians' victorious conquest of the Babylonian armies. Nehemiah served as a "cupbearer" to King Artaxerxes (1:11, 2:1; the same monarch referred to in Ezra 7:1).

As the king's cupbearer, Nehemiah was not required to be a eunuch, but he was nevertheless the taster of the royal food and as such had close daily contact with the king and his administrators. We can see he had a real "taste" for his job!

At Nehemiah's own request, the Persian king ultimately made him governor of Judah, a position he amazingly held for twelve years. The Bible is silent as to any other events in the rest of his life besides this most-notable achievement.

The events recorded here take place in the "twentieth year of King Artaxerxes" (Nehemiah 1:1; 2:1), which on our calendars would be 445 B.C.E. This was also the age of Pericles in Athens, Greece. Rome was still an unknown place at the time.

God's Word in this situation was conclusively about a man, his deeds, and his courage as he dared to stand in the breach, precisely at the very point where and when he was needed. He heard there was a problem back in his home of Israel.

The narrative begins by noting that it was the month of Kislev in the twentieth year of that Medo-Persian monarch. On our Western calendar, Kislev spans part of November and December.

Nehemiah was in the capital, or the "citadel of Susa," the winter residence of the Persian king (Ecbatana was the city of his summer residence). Susa (or as the Greeks called it, "Shushan"), means "lily," presumably because of the abundance of lilies that grew in that area. It was the capital of the province of Elam (present-day Iran), located some 150 miles (241 km) north of the Persian Gulf. Likewise, the events of the book of Esther will take place in Susa, and it will be where the prophet Daniel will receive his vision of the ram and the goat (Daniel 8:2). This site was excavated at the beginning of the twentieth century. In 1901, the famous Code of Hammurabi was discovered there.

Everything in this book begins with the visit of Hanani, Nehemiah's brother (1:2). Hanani had just returned from Jerusalem, but when Nehemiah questioned him about how the Jews, who had returned from the Babylonian captivity, were doing in the hometown of Jerusalem, the answer he got was a sad one: "Those who survived the [70-year] exile and are back in the province are in great trouble and disgrace" (1:3). Hanani went on to describe, "The wall of Jerusalem is broken down and its gates have been burned with fire" (1:3b). Nehemiah seems surprised and appalled by this report, so it is reasonable to suppose that Ezra 4:12 refers to some partial building of the wall shortly after the first return in 538 B.C.E. that had possibly been destroyed by Rehum and Shimshai (Ezra 4:23). Nebuchadnezzar had destroyed the walls in 586 B.C.E., 141 years earlier (2 Kings 25:8–10). But Ezra had led a group of returnees thirteen years before this event in Nehemiah's life (in 458 B.C.E.), and that group had tried to restore the walls and rebuild the city of Jerusalem (Ezra 4:12–13, 16). But that work had been halted by jealous neighbors and supported by the king's decree (Ezra 4:17–23). The work was stopped, and it seems as if the gates to the city were also burned at that same time.

When Nehemiah heard these things, he "sat down and wept." In fact, "For some days [he] mourned and fasted [as he] prayed before the God of heaven" (1:4b). In our modern day, with the use of long-range, airborne warfare, it is difficult for us to realize how important it was to have a walled city to protect the population. The words "wall" and "walls" are very important—they occur some 32 times in this book, and "to build" appears 23 times. So, this made up one of the central concerns of Nehemiah and all who were like-minded with him.

How does one pick up the pieces after suffering the disgrace and the troubles of an ignominious exile, only to now face a new, further disgrace? The remnant living in a city were exposed to any enemy or attacker now that their wall was again destroyed. As Nehemiah prayed about this issue, God called him to be the leader who would stand in the gap to do something about it. This expression "to stand in the gap" comes from two passages, Psalm 106:23 and Ezekiel 22:30.

> So [God] said he would destroy them—had not Moses, his chosen one, stood in the breach [gap] before him to keep his wrath from destroying them.
>
> I looked for a man among them who would build up the wall and stand before me in the gap on behalf of the land so I would not destroy it, but I found none.

All too many shrink back from the lonely place of leadership, especially in the critical moments in the life of a nation, city, congregation or institution. People look for those who have a sense of what it is they all together must do, but they want this leadership from a visionary, from one who also has a light hand, and from one who is not on an ego trip. There is always a call for servant-leaders who look to their Lord for guidance, handle God's people gently, and regard the men and women to be God's flock and not their own! Here is the first mark of a true leader: He or she is willing to stand in the gap. God's call came because of the enormous need that, up to this point, was not being addressed. It came because of the potential shame that God's name and his people were suffering if no one would stand in the gap.

By Praying for Divine Success – 1:5–11

Nehemiah went on to illustrate the centrality of prayer in this servant-leadership role. Prayer appears twelve times in these thirteen chapters (1:4–11, 2:4, 4:4–5, 4:9, 5:19, 6:14, all of chapter 9, 13:14, 13:22, 13:29, 13:31). Nehemiah thanked God for his divine work in the past (6:16; 9:6, 7, 24, 32, 37; 13:2), in the present (1:8; 4:5, 15), and the work God would do in the future (2:20; 4:20; 13:14, 22, 29, 31).

The lesson here is clear: The greater God becomes in our eyes as we wait on him in prayer, the smaller the problems and issues we face in leadership will become. Our Lord is aware of what is going on and is sovereign over all that takes place in this world, for his power exceeds all the power that sets itself in opposition to him and his plan. Therefore, prayer, like leadership begins with adoration of our majestic and magnificent Lord, and with worship of his awesome person and works.

God is properly addressed as "God of heaven," a phrase commonly used in the Persian Empire. The Persians spoke of their gods similarly. But as used by Nehemiah, it was a shortened form for the God of the heavens and the earth, i.e., the God of all the universe (cf. Genesis 24:3, 7; Psalm 136:26; Jonah 1:9; Daniel 2:18, 19, 37, 44; and Revelation 11:13). Our God is incomparably great, and his transcendent power can be seen over all the universe.

Nehemiah addressed the Lord also as "the great and awesome God," a description Moses used in Deuteronomy 7:27 when he wanted to inspire confidence in the people as the Israelites began to be seized with dread of the Canaanites. He urged, "Do not be terrified by them, for the Lord your God, who is among you, is a great and awesome God." The Hebrew word for "awesome," literally translated "terrible," was used in contexts where God would intervene on behalf of his people, as in the Exodus (Exod. 15:11; 34:11). It is for this reason that God should be "feared," for he alone could make miracles happen for them. He could also act as judge of his own people when they refused to follow him, which they already had and were thus carted off into exile.

Acknowledging God's worthship (i.e., worship), not only gives perspective on problems leaders face, but it also gives comfort to the distressed and those who are befuddled. God's awe-inspiring nature points to his holiness and separatedness, along with his power to affect his will and to work on behalf of those who call out to him in prayer.

God also is the one "who keeps his covenant of love with those who love him and obey his commands" (1:5b). This is not to make a case for meritorious works but for a faith that is steadfastly centered on the Lord. The Hebrew word for "love" in the phrase "keeps his covenant of love" is the *hesed*, used 248 times in the Old Testament (*Tanakh*). No one, two, or more English words can accurately or fully render this wonderful term except "grace." The love of God is the ground and the reason for such strong hope and confidence that he will intervene on our behalf, and the reason why we would want to obey his commands.

So, prayer, like leadership, begins in adoration and worship of such a magnificent Lord. Here is the primary need in most ministries today; all theology and work for God must begin in doxology. Leaders must start with adoration of the living God!

By Pleading for God's Forgiveness Individually and Corporately – 1:6–7

Nehemiah's prayer, like the prayer of all God's servant-leaders, was centered on God's previous invitation to pray as found in the Scripture. In fact, some of the words of Nehemiah's prayer come straight for Solomon's dedicatory prayer in 1 Kings 8:29, 52 (cf. 2 Chronicles 6:20, 40; Psalm 130:2). In 1 Kings 8:29, Solomon prayed, "May your eyes be open toward this temple, night and day, this place of which you said, 'My name shall be there,' so that you will hear the prayer your servant prays toward this place." And in 1 Kings 8:52 Solomon continued to pray, "May your eyes be open to hear your servant's plea and to the plea of your people Israel, and may you listen to them whenever they cry out to you."

Nehemiah's prayer was persistent, for he prayed "day and night" (1:6). This was the content of his steadfast prayer for four months prior to his request of the king to be released from his court duties at court to go fix the problem with the wall of Jerusalem (2:4). Such persistent prayer brings our lives into conformity with God and prepares us to receive God's answer and to carry out his will and plan. Sometimes God will use the very ones he has called to pray about a situation to be the ones who will personally be the ones to answer that prayer.

His prayer, as all leaders' prayers should be, was corporate as well as personal. He identified himself with his people and their need for God's forgiveness of their iniquity and trespasses. He said, "I confess the sins we Israelites, including myself and my father's house, have committed against you. We have acted very wickedly towards you. We have not obeyed the commands, decrees, laws you gave your servant Moses." He did not exclude himself, for all effective prayer must be accompanied by one's own personal confession, as well as the confession for one's family, congregation, nation and institution. Our continued distress is often directly related to the unconfessed sin in the life of the leader and/or the lives of the group to which one belongs. How can there be effective leadership when unforgiven sin exists in the leader or the people?

By Basing Our Requests on God's Word – 1:8–9

Leaders must know how to pray. They must also know what they are to pray for. Prayer is not a heavenly grab-bag in which we treat God as some sort of divine bellhop. Instead, effective prayer must be based on the promises of God. It is for this reason that verse 8 begins, "Remember the instruction you gave your servant Moses, saying, 'If you are unfaithful, I will scatter you among the nations.'" God had clearly warned that disobedience would bring disaster (Leviticus 26:14–39; Deuteronomy 28:15–68)—and it did! But the purpose of God's punishment was always to bring his people back to himself.

Nehemiah quotes from memory Deuteronomy 4:27 and 28:64, where God had warned that he would scatter his people if they turned from him. That was true at the time of the exile Israel experienced, and it was a result of their disobedience to the Word of God. It was also true that God's promises were just as dependable as the people were being undependable. The reality of the punishment led all who listened to trust the reality of the promise of a restoration to the land in the grace of God.

Thus, verse 9 gave the promise that even if the people were dispersed all over the world, to the "farthest horizon," God would "gather them from there and bring them to the place [he] had chosen as a dwelling for his name." The Lord God had chosen Zion/Jerusalem as his resting place forever (Deuteronomy 30:1–5; Psalm 132:13–14), and that is why Jerusalem would be "sanctified forever" (2 Chronicles 30:8). That is the place the Lord had chosen (Psalm 68–69), and that is where he would make his name known (Jeremiah 7:11). Other prophets appealed to the same idea—Isaiah 2:2–4; Zechariah 1:14; 2:12.

It may seem strange for Nehemiah to be praying for a return of his people to the land of Israel when about 50,000 of them were already back. But instead of his praying for the removal of their reproach and affliction, in this context Nehemiah does not focus on the divine compassion as much as he does on the righteousness and faithfulness of a covenant-keeping God.

But notice how God's servant-leader appeals to the Word of God, not to his own strategies or abilities, to effect what needs to be done. Nehemiah's words were the very words Moses used to plead with God on Mt. Sinai (Deuteronomy 9:29) at the very point where Israel had been threatened with extinction. Remember, however, it is not God's leader (Moses in this case) who was more lenient than God. He had prepared his leader for just such a time and just such an activity as this—to stand in the gap and to plead for God's special grace in a perilous situation. And that is how he was preparing Nehemiah and all who follow in their way in our day as well.

By Importuning God to Show We Understand the Value of What We Ask For – 1:10–11

Verse 10 is almost an identical copy of Deuteronomy 9:29. An analogy is drawn between God's work of redemption at the Exodus from Egypt and the work that is called for in this new situation in the Persian court. Whereas that earlier redemption was from the physical oppression of the Egyptians, now it would involve a deliverance from the power and judgment of sin by a wonderful redeemer (Jeremiah 1:18; Revelation 5:9, 14:3–4), That is how the "great strength" and "mighty hand" of God would be seen (v. 10). God's mighty hand and power had been evidenced in his deliverance of that nation from Egypt (Deuteronomy 7:8; 9:26, 29), and now in its deliverance from Babylon. But there was more to God's redemption than mere physical deliverance.

Nehemiah's delight was in "revering [God's] name" (v. 11). As in the book of Malachi, they "thought on the name of the Lord" (Malachi 3:16). That is what characterized them—for as a person thinks in his heart and mind, so he or she is. God wanted his leader to offer this prayer over the four months he waited to show him (and by extension, us) the value of what we ask for. Just as parents do not give in to every whim and fancy their children express as they go through the toy department, with their child yelling, "I want that and that and that," they wait to see if in subsequent weeks, the child still remembers the particular toy before they will purchase that item. If we are wise in doing so, how much wiser is God as he waits to see how important the requests are to each of his leaders?

There was also a sense of urgency, for Nehemiah asked God to grant success "today." The four months of prayer must have been nearing an end. He felt it was the right time to act as he posed the question to the king. But that permission would come from God, not from his human leader.

Napoleon and his favored generals would stand to the side of a battle and watch how it developed before determining what would be the key to victory and entering the fray. In like manner, servant-leaders must wait on the Lord to see how the battle shapes up, for the battle is the Lord's and not ours. Leaders are rarely if ever born; they are formed in the gracious providence and school of the Lord. Are you one such leader God is presently shaping? Are these the tools you are using or would use if called to be a leader?

Conclusions

1. God calls today for new leaders to stand in the widening gap, to experience some of the crying needs of our day, to sense the width of the gap, and to hear that as part of the call.

2. God wants to teach his new leaders how to pray, for unless we have a new perception of who God is and what he is able to do, we will be tempted to go in our own strength and thus fail at being a leader.

3. As leaders, we must implore God to forgive our own sin and the sins of our colleagues, congregations, nation, and those we are to lead. To fail to do so is to fail before we start.

4. We must have a new sense of the importance and relevance of the Word of God if we are to lead effectively and with the authority and sufficiency of the Word of God behind us.

Questions for Discussion or Reflection

1. If leadership is often rightly described as being so lonely, why would a person ever wish to volunteer to be a leader in the work of God?

2. What significance does this passage teach us about prayer and quality leadership and what life-habits such would imply?

3. In what sense does the Word of God give direction to the content of our prayers as leaders?

Lesson 2

Achieving Success in Congregational Leadership

Nehemiah 2:1–3:32

The practice of good leadership skills has a long history, especially in biblical times. As far back as the days of Moses, his father-in-law, Jethro, laid out a most amazing leadership course for him in Exodus 18:20–21. Jethro listed four excellent criteria for choosing leaders, and these criteria are still relevant for our day.

First, he suggested, Moses should "select/able men from all the people." Leaders must show aptitude for leadership as distinguished from all the other people in the group. Second, they should be persons "who fear God." Psalm 111 and Proverbs 3 say "the fear of the Lord is the beginning of wisdom," so the leader's life should clearly evidence such fear of God. Third, these selected leaders should be "trustworthy men." Integrity and a record of faithful dependability would be further indicators of the type of person Moses (and we) should look for in potential leaders. Finally, these should be persons "who hate dishonest gain." Those who were subject to taking bribes, or who were looking for ways to enhance their own pockets and fortunes, would not make good leaders at all.

Jethro further advised Moses to "teach [these potential leaders] the decrees and laws" found in the Word of God! Those who have little or no training in the Word, or who lack the skills to work with people, usually will not make good leaders. They ought to be trained in the law of God and how decisions were rendered in actual cases.

Moses would be wise to also teach these new leaders "the way to live." Don't assume that people will automatically know and adopt a believer's lifestyle. Mentoring of leaders, and how they can mentor others, must actually be taught; rarely is it just something that is "caught." They were also to be taught "the duties they are to perform," so that they knew what it was they were expected to do in order to glorify God. Jethro's advice to his son-in-law Moses should become the basic model for all who have the responsibility for training leaders for ministry in a congregation.

Nehemiah 2 and 3 demonstrate how God helped Nehemiah as he went about this task of leading, instructing and developing other leaders for the work of God. Let us examine what the text of Scripture teaches us!

Seek the Evidence of God's Favor and Guidance – 2:1–8, 11–16

Backed by a Life of Prayer

Ever since Nehemiah heard that Jerusalem had been left in ruins after some unspecified attack on her, for about four months Nehemiah continued to pray and mull over all that God had laid on his heart about the burden of Jerusalem's sad state of disrepair and collapse.

During this time, Nehemiah had not mentioned his idea of trying to rejuvenate Jerusalem to the king or to anyone else while he continued to serve as the king's official "cupbearer." On the American calendar, Nehemiah's four months of prayer would have been from Thanksgiving (November) until Passover/Easter in March/April. All that time he had been praying and planning what he would do if the opportunity arose. Good leadership always involves good planning and fervent praying. In fact, it is during those times of prayer and careful planning that God lays special insights on the hearts and minds of leaders.

It was Nehemiah's duty to taste the wine whenever some was brought to the king. It was also mandatory that the "cupbearer" not be sad in the king's presence, for that would signal that something was not right. The position of cupbearer was one of honor and influence, with special access to the royal court. In Persian artistic representations, this person is shown as next in rank to the crown prince attending to the king.

But on one occasion, which Nehemiah likely planned, he allowed his sadness to be evident to the king, immediately alerting him that something might be wrong. "Why does your face look so sad when you are not ill?" the king inquired. "This can be nothing but sadness of heart" (v. 2). When Nehemiah replied that his ancestral city was in ruins. The king asked, "What is you want?" (v. 4a). This was the precise moment and type of questioning Nehemiah had prayed for.

Nehemiah quickly sent up an emergency silent prayer to God as he took a moment before answering the king. That is, Nehemiah had immediate access to the throne of God by means of his silent prayer. Yes, this is the moment for which he had been seeking God in prayer for these past four months; in fact, this had been his prayer ever since he heard of the run-down, decrepit state of affairs Jerusalem's security was now in.

It is significant, again, to note the immediacy of access that Nehemiah felt he had into the courts of heaven by prayer. He did not wait until he was in the Temple precincts, nor did he suddenly turn toward the east to offer his prayer, nor did he spread out a prayer rug to kneel on, or anything like that. He just quietly lifted his heart in prayer. He believed God would hear him and answer. Such quick or sentence-prayers were valid because they had the background of the months of private prayer that had gone before this spontaneous prayer was quickly lifted to heaven.

This was Nehemiah's first departure from his normal happy demeanor in his continued service to the king as "cupbearer." But the inner struggle that had been going on for those past four months had burned a deep desire within him to see the name of the Lord vindicated, as the holy city of Zion and its walls and gates were restored back to their former state.

So finally, on that day, Nehemiah's countenance reflected what he had been feeling inwardly. The internal struggle was outwardly manifested in the sorrow on his face. "I had not been sad in [the king's] presence before," Nehemiah tells us (v. 1). Thus, in God's providence, the king saw the marked difference in his demeanor and asked him what was wrong.

Anticipated in the Details of the Request

Nehemiah began by pronouncing a verbal blessing for the longevity of the life of the king: "May the king live forever!" (v. 3a), which was both a common formula in addressing the king and a request to God to bring the blessing. But then Nehemiah immediately launched into his request. No doubt with his heart in his throat, and his voice perhaps shaking a bit, the "cupbearer" began, wisely avoiding mention of the name of the city of Jerusalem. Artaxerxes had already agreed in previous correspondence (Ezra 4:12) that it was a "rebellious city," so there was no need to antagonize him with such a reminder.

Nehemiah's explanation of the reason for his sadness was this: "The city where my fathers are buried lies in ruins, and its gates have been destroyed by fire" (v. 3b). Thus, Nehemiah fixed attention on his respect for his ancestors as well as his sense of shame for the condition of his home-city, rather than focusing on the name of Jerusalem.

Some historians have noted that the rulers of Persia had tremendous respect for the graves of their ancestors, so this concern would strike a chord in the king's own thinking. This certainly was the politically correct way of pointing to his home city without unnecessarily naming it and unwittingly raising a focus on the wrong aspect of the request.

Nehemiah had his request thought out in advance. He asked, "If it pleases the king and if your servant has found favor in his sight, let him send me to the city in Judah where my fathers are buried so I can rebuild it" (v. 5b–c). The king did not turn down the idea right out of hand; instead, as he sat listening to Nehemiah's request with his queen beside him (v. 6a), he inquired further, "How long will your journey take, and when will you get back?" (v. 6b). We are not immediately told Nehemiah's answer to this question. It will not come for a good long time.

Worked Out in a Plan of Execution

King Artaxerxes is generally known from historical sources as the mildest and most generous of all the Persian monarchs—and this proved to be true in this situation as well. The "queen" (here an unusual word, *shegal*, not the normal Hebrew title used for "queen"), who sat beside him, may have been his official queen, Damaspia. The Hebrew word used here is also used in Psalm 45:10 to refer to the chief member of the royal harem. That she is mentioned as being present here may indicate that she favored Nehemiah and helped his case, or at least served as a witness to the king's words to him. While queens did not normally take part in state councils, this was not an official business session but seemed to be part of a meal-time conversation.

As noted, the text does not tell us the answer Nehemiah gave as to how long the work would take and how long he would be gone. Later in Nehemiah 5:14, we learn that Nehemiah was governor in Jerusalem for a total of twelve years. Possibly his original request was for a much shorter period, and he later increased it when he reported back to the king at the time of the dedication of the walls. The Scriptures do not say.

There is good evidence that Nehemiah had planned carefully, for he requested letters from the king for safe passage cross-country as he journeyed to Jerusalem. This letter was addressed to the governors of Trans-Euphrates, along with another letter to Asaph, keeper of the king's "forest," to obtain the timbers needed to make the gates of the city, timbers for the beams to be used for the citadel and the governor's residence he would occupy (vv. 7–8).

The "citadel by the Temple" was the fortress we know about that appeared on the north side of the Temple mount. The north side of the city of Jerusalem was always the hardest to defend since the land leveled off, without any of the valleys that were on the east, south, and west sides. So, this citadel was no doubt the precursor of the later Roman tower known as Fort Antonia.

Whether the trees came from the "forest" that was the same as the fabled forest of Lebanon, as it was for Ezra's needs (cf. Ezra 3:7), or it was in Judah itself, is not clear. But the timber was to be supplied on the king's orders. It would also be used in building the walls, and for the first time, the building of a governor's residence. All of these requests came as a result of Nehemiah's times in prayers over the past months. Thus, we see once again that good planning begins in times of persistent prayer.

Nehemiah was given permission by the king to go to Jerusalem, "because the gracious hand of [his] God was upon him" (v. 8d). He was given a royal escort consisting of "army officers" and a "cavalry" (v. 9c). So, he passed through unobstructed, even though "Sanballat the Horonite and Tobiah the Ammonite official" (v. 10a) were greatly disturbed that anyone "had come to promote the welfare of the Israelites" (10c). Sanballat probably came from one of the cities named Beth-Horon, which were eighteen miles northwest of Jerusalem, and not, as others suggest, from the Moabite town of Horonaim. We know from the Elephantine Papyri that Sanballat was still governor of Samaria in 408 B.C.E., for his sons were acting for him at that time, probably due to his elderly condition. Tobiah was likely governor of Ammon, even though he had a Jewish name. These Tobiads may have been descendants of the Tobiah listed in Ezra 2:60, who "could not show that their families were descendants of Israel," so they were rejected from Israel.

When Nehemiah reached Jerusalem, it seems he rested for three days from his journey, just as Ezra did (Ezra 8:32). Rest is not a bad idea for leaders either! In fact, leaders today should give this idea of a time of rest serious consideration in the work of God! Having rested, Nehemiah got to work. But first he needed to survey the project and lay out his final plans.

Without attracting attention, he went with a single mount at night as he exited the city of Jerusalem by the "Valley Gate," considered to be the chief gate in the western wall overlooking the Tyropean Valley. That gate has now been found in excavations. Up to this point in this narrative, he still "had not told anyone what God had put into his heart to do for Jerusalem" (v. 12b).

He went toward the "Jackal Well" (v. 13a), likely near En-rogel, but we are not exactly sure. He proceeded to the southernmost portion of the city to the "Dung Gate" (v. 13b), where the Tyropean and Hinnom Valleys meet, all the time examining the state of the collapsed and burnt walls. He then went to the "Fountain Gate" (v. 14a) on the southeast side of the city, where was so much debris that he could not proceed on his mount, so he turned around and retraced his steps and reentered the unfortified city by the Valley Gate (v. 15b). Neither the "Officials" nor the "Jews, or the priests, or the nobles" knew where he had gone or what he was up to (v. 16).

Win the Confidence of Those You Will Lead – 2:9–10, 17–20

By Informing and Exciting the Workers about the Task at Hand

Nehemiah was a master at knowing when and how to present the building project. When he did present it to the people of the land, he used four incentives (v. 17):

1. He spoke of the "trouble *we* are in," thus identifying himself with the people.
2. He pointed to the reality of the situation as he rehearsed the fact that the city currently laid in ruins and its gates had been burned.
3. He called for the people to join him in building the walls.
4. He showed how God had so far favored the project in that the king had generously agreed to let him initiate this task (v. 18).

God's leaders who hear of real needs in the community always should be the first to lead in prayer. However, often God calls those very same persons not only to pray for the project but to be part of the solution as well. That is what Nehemiah did in this case.

By Laying the Basis of Our Calling Before All the People

The strongest appeal this leader could make was to be found in the "gracious hand of God" upon his calling. When God rests his favor on a project, it has the success of heaven behind it. So, Nehemiah pointed to the favor the Persian king had granted him as a sign that God was in this project.

That was the sign Nehemiah gave the people. If they did not believe his word had come from God, how could anyone explain what the king had done? He had the king's letters in his hand, which also addressed how they would get the necessary materials to build the walls, the gates, the citadel, and a governor's residence. What more did they need to begin?

The people replied, "Let us start rebuilding" (v. 18c). And so they did!

By Refusing to Be Intimidated by the Opposition

Sanballat, Tobiah and Geshem the Arab were really the bad dudes in this project, determined to do everything they could to stop any walls or building being raised to the glory of God. When they heard about these plans and the people's willingness to rally to this cause, they were deeply disturbed and violently opposed to the whole idea. They "mocked and ridiculed us" (v. 19b), the text tells. Immediately, they started the rumor that the people were "rebelling against the king" (v. 19c)—a real case of "fake news."

But Nehemiah, through his days and weeks of prayer, was ready for them. He answered coolly and calmly with this declaration: "The God of heaven will give us success. We his servants will start rebuilding, but as for you, you have no share in Jerusalem, or any claim, or even any historic right to it" (v. 20). Success could be counted on for the Jewish settlers because God had put the thought into the heart and mind of the person he had called to lead.

Demonstrating Good Principles of Leadership – 3:1–32

Nehemiah proceeded with his strategy to rebuild the walls. Chapter 3 records 42 detailed sections of the work he assigned. The jobs were handed out, moving counterclockwise around the wall section by section, starting with the Sheep Gate (v. 1) near the northeast corner of the city wall and going all the way around the city back to the Sheep Gate again (v. 32).

There were four formulas for success Nehemiah used here: Coordination of the Effort, Cooperation of All Involved, Convenience of Those Involved, and Commendation of the Workers. Each of these formulas will be considered as we draw the principles for good leadership from this chapter and note how these same principles can be applied today!

Coordination of Effort

Fourteen times the phrase "next to him" (Hebrew *'al yado*) was used as the workers were made conscious that they were all parts of one and the same body and therefore they had to function smoothly (3:2, 4, 5, 7, 8, 9, 10, 12, 17, 19). In a similar way, another phrase emphasized the need for coordination, for fifteen more times it stressed "next to him," "beyond him" (Hebrew *'aharyo*; 3:16, 17, 18, 20, 21, 22, 23, 24, 25, 27, 29, 30, 31). Nehemiah knew where each person would work and how each fit into the whole plan God had given him.

The task of leaders, however, was to make sure the work was totally coordinated and to ensure the whole project received equal attention and could be brought to a smooth conclusion. Just as a chain is no stronger than its weakest link, so a wall was no stronger a source of defense than its weakest section. That all called for coordination of all involved.

Cooperation of All

This work of rebuilding the wall would not be successful if the working class, or the poor, were the only ones doing the work. Nehemiah had to see that all the members from all walks of life were given an opportunity to use their gifts. So he saw to it that priests, Levites, gatekeepers, rulers (3:15–16), goldsmiths (3:31, 32, 8), merchants (3:32), Temple servants (3:26), and pharmacists/perfume makers (3:8) were all equally involved in the work. It even included "the help of one man's daughters" working on the wall (3:12).

Not everyone joined in, however. There will always be naysayers. In this case it was the nobles of Tekoa, who "would not put their shoulders to the work under their supervisors" (v. 5b). But that was no reason to halt the work; the work must go on despite the negativity and unwillingness of some to lift a finger or to give a hand.

It is also important to note that the workers came not only from Jerusalem but also from the outlying towns of Jericho, Tekoa, Gibeon, Mizpah, Zenoah, Beth Haccherem, Beth-Zur and Zelah. When things got dangerous, a guard had to be posted on the job around the clock, to protect those from the outlying towns who were ordered to stay day and night in Jerusalem while the project was underway.

Convenience of Those Involved

Nehemiah did not have people commuting to work all over the city of Jerusalem, but instead he capitalized on the interest each would have in building that portion of the wall adjacent to their own homes. In this way they would be working to protect their own homes and families.

This introduced simplicity into the work, but it also meant they would see that it was done correctly so their home and family would not be the weak spot where a break in the wall could occur. Thus, the phrase "in front of," or "opposite his house/room" (Hebrew *neged betam, neged nishkato*), was used to indicate the proximity of their work to the place where many of them lived (3:23, 28–29).

Putting people to work right where they lived was indeed a great leadership principle. If one has trouble working in one's own backyard, so to speak, how will they ever answer the call of God to some other part of the work of God? Jeremiah 12:5 stated the same principle with a metaphor: "If you have raced with men on foot and they have worn you out, how can you compete with horses?"

Commendation of the Workers

Not only did the workers persist day and night in the labors given to all of them, but several who finished their assigned section on the wall took another section of the wall as well. This can be seen in Nehemiah 3:11, 19, 20, 24 and 30.

You can be sure this spirit of going the extra mile not only gladdened the heart of the leader Nehemiah, but it also lifted the spirits of the other workers. Good leaders use praise where praise is legitimately required, for believing leaders follow the Apostle Paul's example; he gave thanks for the Philippian believers for "every remembrance" of them (Philippians 1:3).

In a former day, some interpreters had wanted to read the preceding section Nehemiah as allegorical. But there is no indication that the names of the gates in Jerusalem are anything other than real names for real gates. For example, some taught that the sheep gate suggested the cross and the lamb of God, while the fish gate suggested that God would make us fishers of men (Matthew 4:19). The valley gate symbolized humility (Psalm 84:6) and the dung gate spoke of cleansing from defilement (1 John 1:7–9).

You get the idea; it was an attempt to get a spiritual message from what appeared on the surface to be otherwise, but the Bible was really talking about what was a historical, secular, and material passage and the rebuilding of a real wall. But the principles we have noted here are formulas for success. They are indeed spiritual if used to instruct the congregation how to incorporate the same principles in the service of the house of God. Those principles are divine and are of great use to God's people.

Conclusions

1. No congregational leader can be successful without a life of prayer. There is a real relationship between the time of prayer for each message delivered and the amount of success realized!

2. Leadership demands organizing skills along with good people skills.

3. Changing hearts and attitudes towards a leader, or the work to which God has called him, is genuinely the work of God; therefore, these leaders must also be the objects of special prayer as are the persons to whom he or she speaks.

4. Leadership must begin in the fear of God, or it will soon just become another job.

Questions for Discussion of Reflection

1. What principles of good leadership, which Moses learned from his father-in-law Jethro, are especially relevant today?

2. Does God's work always face opposition as demonstrated by the trio of objectors in this story with their complaints? What is to be counter to such objectors?

3. How does Nehemiah exhibit wisdom in the way he assigns the work of the wall?

4. Which of the four principles he used impressed you the most?

5. Can you think of parallel situations in your congregation or business and show how you managed or failed to meet these properly?

6. What are leaders to do when not everyone likes them or the tasks they have set before the group?

7. Dare we begin a new task without first having a time to plan in our prayer time how we can carry out that task?

8. How will it be evident that the work of leadership you are involved in is in accord with the plan of God?

9. How can we apply Jethro's piece of advice on choosing and training leaders for the work of God?

Leading While Under Pressure from the Outside

Nehemiah 4:1–23

It is not altogether unusual for leaders to encounter opposition to some of the many projects to which they have been called. This is especially true of those causes that seem to run counter to the wishes of those on the outside of the group such leaders have been called to lead. And when it comes to the work of God, we can almost automatically expect that the Evil One will trigger some sort of opposition or hostility from external sources, if not eventually from internal sources as well. But God is greater than all the opposition; he is the "great and awesome God."

In this case, Sanballat, the governor of Samaria, and his associates exemplify that very type of opposition to the work God had called Nehemiah to. When they heard that Nehemiah was starting to rebuild Jerusalem's walls, they got all stirred up and immediately initiated a campaign of ridicule and innuendo to halt the project. Even though Sanballat was governor of another province up north in Samaria, he thought he could, or at least should, control Jerusalem as well (2:10, 19). Nehemiah, on the other hand, prayerfully placed his case in God's hands (4:4, 14, 19–20, 22). This is the most important contrast in this passage! So let us look at the exposition of this chapter.

For Ridicule There Is Divine Retribution – 4:1–6

The greatest test a leader faces usually comes in the heat of a crisis. How he reacts to that opposition either makes or breaks him. Nehemiah 4 lists several forms of opposition the leader faced, recorded for the benefit of future leaders who trust the same Lord to instruct them as to how they should respond in times such as these. Nehemiah, under God's direction, exhibited precisely what a dedicated, faithful, wise, and energetic leader must do when the opposition comes from outside of one's own group.

Apparently, the progress on the construction of the fallen city walls had reached its halfway mark (v. 6). To derail this project, Sanballat, governor of Samaria, and Tobiah, the Ammonite, really began to put pressure on the confidence of the people and their leader.

Sanballat knew a restored Jerusalem would diminish his influence in the area, so he was really angered by the whole project. This response is not unusual to the work of God, regardless of where it might be located or the nature of the project. So the enemy engaged in a sort of psychological warfare and resorted to ridicule, which he hoped would be enough to stifle the spirit and the drive the Jewish workers off the wall (pun intended).

Sanballat's ridicule took the form of five rhetorical questions in verse 2. First, he insensitively and snidely asked, "What are those feeble Jews doing?" Now the Jewish people knew they were "frail/feeble" and that this job was more than any one of them would normally have undertaken. Most probably were not used to such hard, manual work, such as lifting heavy stones and raising them to great heights without any power tools.

This workforce also represented all sorts of workers in a long list of professions. Few were actually masons by trade. Moreover, they may not have been in great physical shape to do this type of labor, day after day. In that sense, they were indeed "feeble" and "frail" as their enemies charged. But Sanballat was not the right one to remind them of such inadequacies, for he was neither Jewish nor responsible for the people of Judah.

Sanballat next wanted to instill doubts on the wisdom of such a project, for he asked secondly, "Will they restore their wall?" If they were not masons by trade, what kind of wall could one expect from such novices? In Sanballat's eyes they were just plain incompetent for such a task.

A third rhetorical question (v. 2) asked, "Will they offer sacrifices?" Sanballat was questioning their religious motives, implying these foolish wall-builders were thinking that by prayer and sacrifice they could make the wall grow. Just because the Jewish people regarded this project as a sacrosanct or religious work, how would that help them overcome the odds they were facing, scoffed Sanballat? The Jewish people, Sanballat and Ammon sneered, would never succeed in such a monumental task.

Sanballat's scornful tone continued a fourth time as he jeered, "Will they finish in a day?" These poor masons had no idea of the enormity of the project. They would not have enough energy or strength to keep up this pace day after day, month after month, and maybe year after year—or so he inferred. They had picked a project far beyond them, he jokingly opined.

The fifth and last rhetorical question was, "Can they bring the stones back to life from the heaps of rubble—burned in intense fire as they had been?" Nehemiah, and the crews he had assembled, were dealing with burnt limestone building blocks that the fire had left cracked, chipped, broken and severely damaged. The materials were worthless ("lifeless") for building strong walls, so why put all that energy and effort into a wall that could easily topple over, the opposition continued to mock. The intimidation of the workers by Sanballat and his associates was fierce to say the least. They were clear: "There will be no wall!"

An Ammonite named Tobiah joined in mocking and ridiculing the people's efforts. He claimed the wall was so weak that if an animal as small as a fox should climb up on the wall, it would collapse (v. 3). But this was hyperbole and bluster, for remnants of Nehemiah's wall have been found in archaeological excavations up to this day. It was about nine feet thick. It would take some kind of huge fox to topple that wall! Nevertheless, Tobiah ruthlessly mustered as much disdain as he could to dampen the spirits of the workers on the wall and to undermine Nehemiah's leadership and goals.

What is a leader to do in times such as these? The first thing Nehemiah did was to turn to God in prayer against his enemies. He prayed, "Hear us, O our God, for we are despised. Turn their insults back on their own heads. Give them over as plunder in a land of captivity. Do not cover up their guilt or blot out their sins from your sight, for they have thrown insults in the face of the builders" (vv. 4–5). Nehemiah's prayer has much in common with the Psalms of Imprecation, or even with passages in the prophet Jeremiah, such as Jeremiah 18:23.

There is no need to be embarrassed by Nehemiah's prayer, for he does not work his own wrath or anger on his enemies. He calls on God to intervene. Moreover, it is a prayer of great urgency asking God to help them. Their hands were full of the work God called them to do on the wall. However, some say this prayer does not match Matthew 6:12–13, "Forgive us our debts as we also have forgiven our debtors, and lead us not into temptation, but deliver us from the evil one."

Others have tried to rescue the good name of the Bible and its leaders by unhelpfully saying this story only records what Nehemiah prayed for and does not teach that we should do the same.

Or it is said that this only shows the excitable Near Eastern mentality and the verbs should not be taken as imperatives but as predictive verbs. The most common way those believers improperly seek to answer such a problem is to appeal to the alleged discontinuity and break between the Old and New Testaments.

Some incorrectly and improperly associate the "love" principle exclusively with the New Testament, thinking that part of the bible has higher moral principles than the Old. But they forget that the theology of "love," as quoted in Luke 10:27–37, Romans 13:9 or Galatians 5:13–14, actually comes from the antecedent theology found in Leviticus 19:18. Thus, there is no discontinuity on the theme of "love" between the Testaments despite this popular misconception and the consequent forced division between the messages of the Old and New Testaments.

None of these answers show any sound thinking, for this text shows how serious it is to deprecate God's work and mock God this way. Therefore, it is a serious offense against God to demoralize his people when they are about his work. Note how 1 Corinthians 3: 16 uses the plural form of the pronoun "you." It warns in effect: "Mess with God's people and God will mess with you." The same theology can be found in Ezekiel 25: 6-7.

> For this is what the Sovereign LORD says: Because you clapped your hands and stamped your feet, rejoicing with all the malice of your heart against the land of Israel, therefore I will stretch out my hand against you and give you [Ammon] as plunder to the nations and exterminate you from the countries. I will destroy you, and [then] you will know that I am the LORD.

The same warning and judgment can be found in Zephaniah 2:8–9.

> I have heard the insults of Moab and the taunts of the Ammonites, who insulted my people and made threats against their land. Therefore, as surely as I live, declares the God of Israel, surely Moab will become like Sodom, the Ammonites like Gomorrah – a place of weeds and salt pits, a wasteland forever. The remnant of my people will plunder them; the survivors of my nation will inherit their land.

Reinforced by the power of prayer, Nehemiah forged ahead on the wall as it reached half of its ultimate height. Even more assuring was this fact: "The people worked with all their hearts" (v. 6b). Thus, one of the principles of leadership is this: Overcoming opposition lies in our relationship to the Lord. Worry can only sap our strength, and fighting the opposition, can only detract us from the work God has given us to do.

For Hostile Alliances There Is Divine Assistance – 4:7–14

When Sanballat and his associates realized their ridiculous ridicule was not working, they began to plot together to force a work stoppage by outright violence. The forces of these enemies literally surrounded the Jewish people: Sanballat's Samaria, of course, was to the north of Judah; Tobiah the Ammonite was on the east side of Judah; the Philistine territory of Ashdod, to Judah's west, had been a separate province ever since the Assyrians conquered Palestine; and the Arabs were to Judah's southeast. It would seem Nehemiah and his wall-builders were surrounded on all sides and doomed to destruction if they persisted in their plan to rebuild the walls.

Nehemiah's response was to pray to God for his protection. He also "posted a guard day and night to meet this threat" (v. 8b). That did not prevent him from taking the necessary human precautions of setting up guards round the clock. Some would have thought such a meager force of workers against so many opposing enemies was more of a joke than a practical solution. But prayer and precaution are not antithetical, and faith and good management are not opposites.

Suddenly, God's leader was faced with an internal complaint: The workers murmured, "The strength of the laborers is giving out, and there is so much rubble that we cannot rebuild the wall" (v. 10). Nehemiah was faced with a potential internal work-stoppage as the people began to echo Sanballat's jeering charges. If ever a leader was tempted to quit, it was in just such a time as this for Nehemiah. A leader can face opposition from the outside, but what is he to do when the people he is trying to serve are opposing him? Discouragement like this can spread like wildfire, and it can put the damper on almost anything being attempted—good or bad.

As if that weren't enough, their enemies began to spread rumors that an assault was looming against the workers (v. 11). With unwarranted bravado, Nehemiah's enemies threatened to fall upon the workers before they could even see them coming and kill them on the spot (v. 11b). This didn't help the stress that the threatened revolt had already put on God's leader.

A third punch came in verse 12; the Jewish people living near the enemies reported some "ten times" that such a surprise attack was about to fall on the workers. What does a leader do about rumor after rumor that is set to shake the unity, stability and drive of those he is trying to lead? It is not easy at all!

But Nehemiah, undeterred by such threats, "stationed some of the people behind the lowest points of the wall, at the exposed places, posting them by their own families, with their swords, spears, and bows" (v. 13) to be ready for an attack. Rather than moaning about the impossible situation God had gotten him into, Nehemiah showed organizational spunk and initiative.

Moreover, he posted the defenders in groups by families. By doing so, he strengthened the resolve and motivation of the defenders to fight for their families. The family was still the basic unit of Israel, which went back as far as the period of Moses and Joshua (Exodus 6:14; Joshua 7:16–18). As the swords, spears and bows were distributed, one could imagine the delight that would come to the builders on the wall as they shouted back and forth to the defenders in lively conviviality and encouragement of each other. This had to be a real morale-booster. They were making some real progress!

However, as Nehemiah "looked things over" (v. 14a), he gathered the people together and "stood up" and spoke to the "nobles, the officials, and the rest of the people: "Don't be afraid of them, Remember the Lord, who is great and awesome, and fight for your brothers, sons, daughters, wives and homes" (v. 14c). "Our God will fight for us" (v. 20c), so the men of Israel could fight for their own relatives and homes. The greater God grew in their minds and hearts, the less threatening the problems they faced. Who could compare to this awesome and great God? Not one person—not one! And to call for "rememb[rance] was more than a mere cognitive act, for in Hebrew it often meant not only to first call something to mind, but it also implied that one would act on it. Thus, when the Lord "remembered Hannah" in 1 Samuel 1, she became pregnant!

For Constant Vigilance There Is Divine Overruling – 4:15–23

When the enemy learned their plots had been disclosed to the workers and that "God had frustrated [their plans]" (v. 15b), the people were able to return to the main task of building the wall. God is able to frustrate the plans of those who work against the leaders he puts into place. There is divine work overruling the events of history.

Thus, it was not about men, force, military strategy, or the brilliance of mortals; it was about God and his awesomeness. The only thing left for the leader to do was to give thanks and praise to the great and awesome God.

Once again God's leader takes a proactive stance as he is more determined than ever to complete the work he has been sent to accomplish.

First, he gave a clear job description to all "my [his] men" (v. 16a). Each was given a specific task (vv. 16–18). Second, he set up clear lines of communication, for in the event of an attack, the trumpeter (shofar-blower), who stayed at Nehemiah's side (v. 18c), was to sound off a blast, signaling the people to gather together around their leader for instructions. Third, Nehemiah extended the working hours "from the first light of dawn until the stars came out" (v. 21b). In this way they could complete the project sooner than anticipated. Fourth, he instituted a new rule: "Have every man and his helper stay inside Jerusalem at night, so they can serve us as guards by night and workmen by day" (v. 22a).

Nehemiah was a great team builder. His team consisted of men and brothers. The officials seemed to be those who had returned with him from Persia, and whom Nehemiah expected to join with him in the work he had been commissioned by the Persian monarchy to accomplish.

In this manner, Nehemiah was able to meet the opposition that came from external sources. Such is a model for all other servants of God who aspire to the role of leadership. God will fight for them just as he fought for Nehemiah and his men.

Conclusions

1. Often the work of God goes forward under pressure from forces outside of the people of God. Leaders can be assured that they will be garrisoned about by the presence and power of God if they call on him and depend on him in prayer.

2. Gigantic odds are nothing for an awesome God. For what person, group, or combination of problems is any match for God?

3. The best-laid plans of opposition boomerang on those who oppose God's leaders or work. The opponents themselves become his targets.

4. Blessed is the believing group to whom God gives a mind and a heart to work and to do what he has shown them to do.

Questions for discussion or Reflection

1. How is crass ridicule pressure against godly leadership? What can be done to face it and resolve it?

2. Why is opposing the work of God equal to opposing the Lord himself? What can be done about such attacks, and how can they be met?

3. How can hostile alliances against God's work and leaders be defeated?

4. Is human vigilance to be avoided in favor of depending solely on God?

5. What is a leader to do when opposition begins to build inside the group of those he is attempting to lead?

Lesson 4

Leading While Under Pressure from the Inside

Nehemiah 5:1–19

It is enough for leaders to face an adversary on one front, from the outside, but Nehemiah also faced another adversary: He had internal troubles and opposition as well.

This time the problem was centered on the people of Judah themselves—the very ones Nehemiah was attempting to lead! The poorer persons in the community did not have enough food to sustain themselves, while exorbitant interest was being charged by their own people, harvests were dwindling, and a drought of severe proportions was in progress. All of this was happening while the wall around the city of Jerusalem, using the burnt rubble from the collapse of the previous city's wall, was being erected. One major crisis was enough, but several at the same time?

It was time for the new governor, Nehemiah, to step up to the plate. Not only did he have to solve these problems, he had to deal with the wealthy loan-sharks, who were buying up mortgages with no regard for the poor, instead of showing kindness to one another, especially those of their own households! Let's see how Nehemiah handled these crises.

Helping Those Beyond Self-Help – 5:1–5

Apparently, the inequities and injustices in Judah had been going on for some time prior to Nehemiah's arrival. Now, the wall-building, and the external opposition to it, had put an additional strain on the economy, but it also contained the seeds of its own destruction if it were left alone.

The whole issue seems to have come to a head just before the wall was finished in August-September of that year. This would have been near the end of the harvest season, and the creditors would have been requiring payment of interest on the money they had loaned for that crop-year.

As a result, a "great outcry" went up from the men and their wives against "their Jewish brothers" (5:1). All the men were needed for the work on the wall, so the women had to bring in the harvest. The Hebrew word for "outcry" is the same word used to describe the reaction of Israel to their Egyptian oppressors in Exodus 3:9.

Included in this word was one of the most heinous evils, as one member of the human race exploited another by economically oppressing them. Instead of seeing that justice was given to all, here even their own blood brothers were pouncing on them to get all they could get in a get-rich-quick scheme. It was not Nehemiah they charged with this sin but their fellow countrymen, who were of their own flesh and blood, citizens of Judah.

This charge of injustice contained three ancient and familiar complaints that afflict every age and most people on earth: hunger, debts and taxes.

First, in verse 2, there were the wage-earners who were becoming destitute even while they were fully engaged in work. During the time they all were working on the wall, they were unable to produce enough grain for their large families. They had to buy grain, even though they were poor. In addition to this complication, there had been a "famine" (v. 3b). With money scarce, so too was food.

A second set of troubles came from landowners, who in order to buy grain had to mortgage their property (vv. 3–4). The Babylonians had a policy of heavily taxing their real estate—a policy the Persians continued and even increased to as high as 50%. So many Judahites had fallen into the hands of loan sharks, who in turn had made enormous profits. The situation was critical. In fact, when Alexander, the Greek monarch, conquered Susa, one of the Persian capitals, he found some 270 tons of gold and 1200 tons of silver stored away![1] Some of that had to be Jewish tax money!

---

1. A. T. Olmstead, *History of the Persian Empire* (Chicago: University Press, 1948), 297–99.

The most serious complaint, however, was this: The people of Judah were mortgaging their children for food, mortgaging their property, and going into irreversible debt, actually mortgaging their lives to pay taxes. Although this debt-slavery practice was common in the ancient Near East, the Mosaic laws controlled it (Exodus 21:1–11). These same laws also required, by order of the Torah and contrary to other nations' practice, that Jewish slaves were to be released, debt-free, in the sabbatical year, which came every seventh year (Leviticus 25:39–43).

Moreover, the Mosaic Law provided for lending to the poor for a pledge (Deuteronomy 15:8). As noted, they could use their labor as collateral for six years to procure money since they could not use their property. But lifelong, or permanent, slavery, was forbidden for any Israelite. An evil that crept into this practice was when the sons or daughters of Israel were sold to another nation, in which case these sons and daughters became powerless to gain their freedom and ended up permanent slaves (Deuteronomy 28:32; 2 Chronicles 28:10–11). Such insensitivity stirred Nehemiah, as it should also stir us in our day when we too become insensitive to the needs of the poor in our midst.

Being Angry and Not Sinning – 5:6–13

It is a sign that something has gone seriously wrong in our thinking and living when we can see evil or injustice and have no sense of the wrong and unfairness in it. But Nehemiah clearly did not take these new charges lightly; when he "heard their outcry," he "was very angry" (v. 6a).

Anger is sinful, of course, when we lose control of ourselves (James 1:19–20; Galatians 5:19–20), or when we harbor resentment (Romans 12:17–21) and use anger to get even with those we believe have hurt us. The best work ever done on the problem of anger came in the last half of the third century by a Church Father named Lactantius, in his book *De Ira Dei*, "The Anger of God." He too made the point that passions and emotions were not evil in and of themselves if they were kept under control. In fact, these very same passions and emotions could be avenues of virtue and goodness, as they were for Nehemiah, who acted on these abuses to change things. It is the person who loves the good, Lactantius taught, who thereby hates evil and all forms of injustice and wrong.

Our problem with anger is that we incorrectly define it as Aristotle did: "the desire for retaliation, or to get even with someone; that is to get revenge and possibly do them harm as well." But Lactantius had a better definition of anger: "It is the motion of the soul rousing itself to curb sin." God's anger is never explosive, unreasonable, or inexplicable. Instead, his anger marks the end of indifference to the aroused issue; he will not remain neutral or impartial in the presence of sin.

Here are some of the ways in which leaders (and all others) should handle anger:

1. Don't minimize it and say, "That's just me!"

2. Don't excuse it and say to the aggrieved person, "You made me do it!"

3. Don't repress it and tritely say, "Oh, forget it."

4. Don't project it and say, "Brother, just get out of my way!"

What Nehemiah did in such a situation is exactly what leaders should do: "I pondered them in my mind" (v. 7a). Leaders must take time to carefully consider a matter. The Hebrew literally reads, "My heart *took counsel* on it." This translation of the verb *malak* (normally rendered "to rule, reign") is unusual, but it is also found in Syriac as "to consult," as it is also used in Daniel 4:24, 27. After he had taken counsel from his heart, Nehemiah took action.

He made sure that he knew what the issues were and where the trouble was coming from. Then he "accused the nobles and officials" (v. 7b). The charge he brought was that these wealthier Jews were charging interest for lending money to those in need, instead of helping them, free of charge, as the Pentateuch required; the Law of Moses forbade taking usury (inordinate interest) from fellow Jews or the poor (Exodus 22:25; Leviticus 25:36). The problem was not with the principle of lending, for Nehemiah and his servants did just that (v. 10), but it was scalping them for such high interest rates that it would surely send most of them "to the poorhouse," as we would say—or in their case, into permanent slavery. Nehemiah thundered, "You are exacting usury from your own countrymen!" (v. 7c)

Nehemiah effectively used this situation to call a public meeting, similar to what we call congregational discipline. It takes a bold man to openly face people of such high influence as these loan sharks, especially in troublesome times like these. If these wealthy persons had decided to bolt from Nehemiah's leadership, the unholy trinity of Sanballat, Tobiah and Geshem were right at hand to capitalize on any divisions that may have been caused by internal dissension. Leaders are often put to some of the hardest tests when the unity of the body they are serving is lost and pressures are simultaneously coming from the outside. Which situation does one face first?

His language was friendly. The Hebrew has a grace note not always translated. For example, in verse 10b, Nehemiah said: "*Please*, abandon this practice of usury," and in verse 11a, he urged, "*Please*, return their fields to them this very day." This did not mean he was not also firm; in verse 9, he distinctly stated: "What you are doing is not right. Shouldn't you walk in the fear of our God to avoid the reproach of our Gentile enemies?" Nehemiah also gave some leeway in verse 8, saying "as far as possible"—that is, "according to the means [you] have."

The response could not have been more favorable for this leader. The guilty, wealthy Jews said, "We will give it back. We will not demand anything more from them. We will do as you say" (v. 12). So the payment of a "hundredth part of the money, grain, new wine and oil" (v. 11c), adding up to one percent per month would be dropped for the time being.

No doubt Nehemiah recalled Jeremiah's experience: Everyone agreed to free their own people they had taken into slavery, promising to release them—but soon after, they recaptured them and re-enslaved them (Jeremiah 34:8–11). So, he decided something more official was needed. Accordingly, he summoned the priests to administer an oath, forcing the nobles and officials to publicly vow before the whole assembly that they would keep their word (vv. 12, 13c). The Law of

Moses required that the priests should administer such oaths (Numbers 5:19), and so they did.

For good measure, Nehemiah pronounced a curse on any who would break this oath. He did so by shaking out the folds of his robe (v. 13), just as Paul did in Acts 18:6. This symbolic action said, in effect, may God empty out of his lap all who do not keep what they have promised. Thus, Nehemiah's courageous action bore fruit both with both the offenders, who would now do as they promised, and with those who had suffered badly and unfairly.

Setting an Example in Leading – 5:14–19

What motivated and guided Nehemiah was the "reverence for the Lord" (v. 15d). He had the right to claim a tax from the people, for he had heavy expenses of his own running the government. But he chose not to do so. He voluntarily yielded this right, for tough times called for tough decisions. He did not take a salary for his service to the country! Just as the Apostle Paul waived his right for a living wage to be paid by the Thessalonians after he had ministered so earnestly in their midst (1 Thess. 2:9; 2 Thess. 3:8), Nehemiah had waived a similar right and instead paid, out of his own pocket, all the costs of providing for the 150 Jews who daily ate at his table. So it happens at times in leadership when *lex* is not *rex*—"law is not king." "Earlier governors" (v. 15a) in Judah (the Bible only named two prior governors of Judah: Zerubbabel and Ezra), acted differently, but in the hundred years since the first return, there surely were many other governors who had used their privilege to pay for their leadership.

Nehemiah was guided, as all good leaders must also be, by the "fear of the Lord." Recall: "The fear of the Lord is the beginning of wisdom" (Psalm 111:10; Proverbs 9:10). This reverential awe of God made Nehemiah serious about doing everything to please God (v. 15d).

Nehemiah personally involved himself in the work (v. 16) as he led by example. Leaders must be servants and act with selfless service if they wish to have the respect and esteem of those they lead. Some leaders just go out golfing and phone back from the greens with commands for those who work under them to carry on the work, or to harangue the hard work of others from the safety of sitting behind a desk. But God wanted leaders who would humble themselves and put their shoulders to the work as well.

He also wanted leaders who had good people skills and would treat others as they wished to be treated. Leaders must be alert to resolve problems as soon as they arise, rather than hoping they will just go away. For the correction that is necessary for those problems to be effective, there must be full accountability of the leader to his people and to others as required.

Some criticize Nehemiah's final prayer (v. 19) as indulging in self-glorification (see 13:14, 22, 31). But his is not so much a prayer for God to reward him as it is an emphatic way of stating that he has acted in good faith and from right motives. It demonstrates a confidence that God is the judge of all such matters for those who seek him and his will. Even though Nehemiah did take immediate action when these problems came to his attention, he nevertheless showed he was constantly and totally dependent on God. With God's favor and help, Nehemiah dealt swiftly with internal problems of greed, injustice, and wrongdoing. He also did so with pastoral and compassionate care. He began by dealing with the issues privately (v. 7), but when he learned these were public issues, he called for an assembly of the community to deal publicly with matters that affected the whole group. What a model for leaders today.

Conclusions

1. Isaiah 58:10 informs us that when leaders fail to help those in society who are poor and needy, it hinders their own growth spiritually and blocks the guidance they need from God in order to lead. Moreover, it prevents their prayers from being answered. We too are affected in like manner in congregations today!

2. Those leaders who fear God must not neglect the cries of the weak, needy, and oppressed, for the cries of these folks come up to heaven, and God hears their outcry and will hold leaders responsible.

3. Good leaders set the pace and tone for a group by adopting the servant role to accomplish the goal to which they wish to lead God's people.

4. It is an evil to see wrong and not be angered by it, so long as the anger is the result of God arousing our emotions so we can act to curb sin and wickedness.

Questions for Discussion and Reflection

1. Is anger ever legitimate, and if so, in what circumstances? What are the two main ways anger can be defined?

2. How responsible is a leader to seek the welfare of his or her group? What if they do not carry out this task?

3. Are leaders born or made?

4. Which is more difficult to handle: attacks from outside or attacks from within?

Lesson 5

Handling Personal Attacks Against God's Leader

Nehemiah 6:1–19

Sometimes the opposition against God's leaders and his God is so relentless that there seems to be no end to the ways it continues to come.

If a leader and his work cannot be hindered in one way by the schemes of some opponents, then another way is often tried. But the object is to keep that leader hopping and in constant turmoil! This is what happened to Nehemiah as he neared the final stage in rebuilding the wall of Jerusalem.

Sanballat, Tobiah and Geshem, that unholy trio who were his enemies, switched strategies. They were determined to ensure the wall was never finished, leaving Jerusalem perpetually exposed and vulnerable to attack. This requires a deeper look at four types of opposition and ways to respond.

For Intrigue: There Are God-Given Principles of Discernment and Direction – 6:1–4

God's leaders need to be especially careful in their actions to be divinely guided in difficult times. If leaders are to successfully face the task of filling in the gap that currently exists, they must use those principles that will help them cope with challenges to their leadership.

Within two months, the work on the wall around Jerusalem was coming to a surprisingly speedy conclusion. Nehemiah had not yet "set the doors in the gates" (v. 1c), but there was not one breach left in the entire wall. Nevertheless, without the doors in place in the gates, any kind of attack was still possible. If Sanballat, Tobiah and Geshem were going to be successful in stopping the work, now was the time to bring out their most effective strategies. Thus far, none of their other plans had caused the work to stop or to panic Nehemiah into making some kind of administrative blunder.

So Sanballat sent an urgent message to Nehemiah: "Come, let us meet together in one of the villages on the plain of Ono (v. 2b). Since every one of Sanballat's previous schemes had failed to derail or sidetrack Nehemiah, this hostile neighbor thought it was time to try a type of fraudulent summitry. Without a doubt, Sanballat and his cronies were determined to find a solution that would bring the work to a complete stop. They planned to murder Nehemiah once he was outside the walls of Jerusalem and then profess sorrow over this horrible assault by someone else.

There are times when people invite others to what seems like an innocent peacemaking mission but have their own reasons for wanting to discuss the differences that exist between them. Not all "dialogue," as it's often called, is fruitful for the invited "guest." In this case, it was a ruse to put God's leader on the defensive, if not expose him to outright harm and cause a work-stoppage. Surely, there could be little doubt what the three opposition leaders were up to, given their past performance.

In Psalm 119:104, the psalmist taught, "I gain understanding from your [God's] precepts; therefore, I hate every wrong path." In a similar way, Solomon taught in Proverbs 2:6, "For the LORD gives wisdom; from his mouth come knowledge and understanding." This is where a leader can find God's gift of discernment: It comes from God's revelatory word and from the wisdom he supplies from Scripture.

Sanballat wanted to lure Nehemiah outside the city under the pretense of making peace between them. Ono was about seven miles southwest of Joppa on the coast, but considering his past experience, it was not difficult for Nehemiah to surmise that "they were scheming to harm [him]" (v. 2c). We can imagine Nehemiah saying to this invitation to Ono, "Oh, no!"

Instead, he boldly replied that he was engaged in a great work, so he naturally could not join them (v. 3a). He gave a polite but firm answer. A prideful leader might have gotten a bloated impression of his own importance and talked himself into seeing this as an important opportunity to move into new diplomacy. It might have also been a break from his construction project. But Nehemiah was a leader who focused on the task God had given him. It was his first priority. He also had wisdom from God. This wisdom was a God-given sixth sense that could sniff out where the potential for trouble and great harm lay.

God can indeed give direction to those who face schemes—precisely what Nehemiah faced. Moreover, leaders should never trade a lesser work for God's greater call. Nor should a leader's lazy and complacent attitude be a substitute for dedicated work, for we should "never be lacking in zeal" (Romans 12:11). Instead, "Whatever [they did or were to] work at it with all [their] heart, as [one] working for the Lord, not for men" (Colossians 3:23). No less than wise Solomon counseled, "Whatever your hand finds to do, do it with all of your might [while you are still living]" (Ecclesiastes 9:10).

When God has given his direction, it is not the time to drop that work because of an intrigue or other distraction. Accomplishing what God had intended for them/us to do is job one. Instead, as the hymn teaches, "Rise up, O men of God! Have done with lesser things." To this we can add the words of the psalmist once again:

> [God's] commands make me wiser than my enemies, for they are ever with me. I have more insight than all my teachers, for I meditate on your statues. I have more understanding than the elders, for I obey your precepts. (Psalm 119:98–100)

Sanballat was relentless, for he sent this same invitation to join him in peacemaking talks "four times" over (v. 4a). Each time, however, Nehemiah resolutely held his ground and answered the same way: He was not going to join in any discussions or useless dialogues that would take him away from the work God had given him.

For Innuendo: There Are God-Given Principles of Directness and Determination – 6:5–9

Seeing his summit scheme had failed to get Nehemiah off-balance, Sanballat took a different tactic. A fifth attempt was made in the form of an "unsealed" or "open" letter. In that part of the world, as in ours, an unsealed letter quickly becomes a public document, for any and all who wish to see it can do so. This deliberate act might accomplish its destructive aim. Doing so would make possible that eventually the whole city of Jerusalem would know of its contents by way of the rumor mill. It would be like sending a message on a postcard while on vacation—all would then know we were happily living the life of leisure and freedom at some beach resort.

The contents of Sanballat's letter were damaging to Nehemiah's character and purposes. It was a type of smear tactic that attacked the leader's motives and disparaged his character with derogatory statements. In essence, it questioned his motivation for building this wall. "What's his angle? "Why is he doing all this work?" "Surely he is doing this for something he wants to get out of it."

"It is widely reported," Sanballat's letter began (v. 6a). Our own children in our own home learned how to misuse statistics early on as they solemnly reported, "Everyone in the school has one" (the gift they were pleading for). The pressure of the masses gave way to personal coveting. In Nehemiah's case, not only was it widely reported, but they said they could confidently document the source of this widely held report by noting, "and Geshem says it is true" (v. 6b). Therefore, the real source of this "wide report" was just one man named Geshem, who had obviously invented the whole story, just as much of the news-reporting in our day can be based on slander or false statements.

What was the report? It said the Jews were building the wall because they were planning to revolt against the foreign overlords of that day (vv. 6c–d). This was calculated to capture the attention and authority of the Persian government. After all, Jerusalem had a reputation for revolting against previous sovereign governments, for that is how the opposition had already stopped the work in Ezra's day (Ezra 4:21); it was rumor and hearsay.

The open letter also included the scandalous assertion that Nehemiah was being duplicitous; it charged that he had already appointed prophets who would shortly announce, "There is a king in Judah" (v. 7b). In other words, Nehemiah had a messianic complex and he would see to it that he was installed as the new sovereign over Judah. None of this was in the least bit true, but "a lie can travel halfway around the world while the truth is just getting its boots on," as the famous saying goes.

Amazingly, Sanballat pretended he wanted to help Nehemiah to keep this report from coming to the king's attention, but the truth of the matter was that he had been the primary instigator to see that was exactly what was done. Once again, he urged, "Come, let us confer together" (v. 7d). This man Sanballat had an incredible amount of *chutzpah* (nerve).

Nehemiah's solution was to use the God-given principle of *directness* in his response. He simply but firmly said: "Nothing like what you are saying is happening; you are just making it up out of your head" (v. 8). That was straight-enough talk. Indeed, the whole thing had been made up—presumably with the help of Geshem's futile imagination. All too frequently, people are quick to believe the worst things they can imagine about a leader if they don't him or don't want him to accomplish what he is doing. But that too should be committed to the Lord in prayer.

But that directness was backed up by a firm *determination* to remain on course and not be swayed by any kind of interference. Nehemiah concluded, "They were all trying to frighten us, thinking, 'Their hands will get weak for the work,' and it will not be completed." To counter this, Nehemiah prayed, "Now strengthen my hands" (v. 9). In Psalm 27:1, David had sung, as all leaders should, "The LORD is my light and my salvation—whom shall I fear? The LORD is the stronghold [strength] of my life—of whom shall I be afraid?"

Sanballat wanted Geshem's rumor to sound like Nehemiah had messianic pretensions and was up to treasonous activities as far as the Persian government was concerned. Sanballat didn't really want to see the Persian cause advanced; he just had his own pretensions—and they did not include a neighboring Judean province prospering!

For Intimidation: There Are God-Given Principles of Decisiveness and Demonstration of His Approval – 6:10–19

One day Nehemiah went to visit Shemaiah ("the Lord hears"), son of Delaiah (his father's name appears on an early list of returnees; see Ezra 2:60, Nehemiah 7:62). It is not clear why Nehemiah went to see him when he had steadfastly refused to stop his work to go see anyone else. Verse 10b says Shemaiah "was shut up in his house." Apparently, Nehemiah thought Shemaiah was a true prophet. But in actuality he had sold out to the enemy, and he used his influence to undermine Nehemiah. Why Shemaiah was shut up in his house is never explained, but that too might have been a ruse to get Nehemiah off-guard—another of the unholy trio's traps.

But it quickly became apparent that "God had not sent [Shemaiah]" (v. 12a), for what he proposed would not have been suggested by any true prophet who knew the Word of God. Shemaiah also had "Let us meet" (v. 10c) on the brain, but he boldly proposed they go into the Temple, where they could lock themselves in for protection, as "by night [men] are coming to kill you." But Nehemiah knew right then and there that this guy was a fraud and in his enemies' employ, for only the priests could have access to the interior of the Temple. Similar to the situation of Judah's King Uzziah, known from history, he had been stricken with leprosy for his impudent entrance into the Temple to make an offering. That was how Nehemiah discerned that Sanballat and Tobiah had hired Shemaiah. Knowledge of the Word of God had saved him from certain death.

The idea was to force Nehemiah into a position of compromise; perhaps in this way his enemies could have the excuse that they killed Nehemiah because he had violated the law of God. How sanctimonious and diabolical evil can be when it fails to get its way via traditional methods of intimidation and false persuasion!

The fear of the Lord is to depart from evil, taught Solomon in Proverbs 3:7; that is why it will be well with those who fear the Lord (Proverbs 16:6). Therefore, let all leaders beware: Whenever mortals contradict the plain teaching of the Word of God, they are no messengers of his. The teaching of Deuteronomy 13:15 and 18:20 is very clear on this matter. When someone comes with a word supposedly from God and it runs counter to what God has already said in his Word, that is a lie and is not to be received as part of the divine revelation.

Shemaiah was not the only one acting deviously; the prophetess Noadiah was too (v. 14). There were other prophetesses in the Old Testament who had rendered faithful and true service to God, including Miriam (Exodus 15:20), Deborah (Judges 4:4), another prophet named Huldah, who interpreted the Word of God for King Josiah when the Book of the Law was found on a planned work-day in the Temple (2 Kings 22:14; 2 Chronicles 34:22), and in the life of Isaiah's unnamed wife (Isaiah 8:3). So this was not a gender issue but a truth issue. Meanwhile, "the rest of the prophets ... [were] trying to intimidate [Nehemiah]" (v. 14d). But it was no use; God was with his leader, helping him all the way.

But there was also the God-given principle of a *demonstration* of his approval. As Hudson Taylor and others often said, "God's work done in God's way will never lack God's approval." Amazingly, the work on the wall was completed "on the "twenty-fifth of Elul, in fifty-two days" (v. 15). Praise the Lord. That corresponds to October 2, 445 B.C.E. Elul was the sixth month, starting the calendar with the month of Nisan at Passover time. Some people are so astounded by the completion time that they say it is too good to be true. Josephus, the first-century Jewish historian, said it took "two years and four months" (*Antiquities*, XI, 5. 8), but he had no evidence for his assertion and scholars suspect a scribal error.[1] It is best to take Nehemiah's word for it, just as it appears in the best texts of Scripture.

It must not be overlooked that the people "worked with all their heart" (4:6), or as the Authorized Version put it, they "had a mind to work." Add to this the supernatural blessing God had shown to this project from the very start, and there is another factor to be added in the speed with which the work was accomplished. Note as well that there

---

1. It is amazing, however, that most secular historians will take Thucydides' history (1:89–93), in which his word is that the wall around Athens was built in one month!

was a large workforce; they came from all the outlying villages rather than merely from Jerusalem. And the ruins of the previous wall lay at their feet as these large quantities of stones were re-employed once again to form the wall.

One would think that by now the unholy trio of Sanballat, Tobiah and Geshem would have had enough and seen that what God's people had accomplished was nothing less than the hand of God. The timing of this last attempt to dislodge God's leader is not certain, for it simply says "Also, in those days" (v. 17). This may well have been going on throughout the whole period rather than merely just after the wall was finished. Nevertheless, it does seem this matter remained an ongoing problem, as it is noted just after the notice of the completion of the walls in verse 15.

There continued to be a letter-writing campaign between the nobles of Judah and Tobiah, a staunch opponent of the building of the wall. What came out was a long list of praises for the good deeds and character of Tobiah, despite his opposition to the main project of those days. Some of these folks were close allies of his, for they had pledged allegiance to him due to marital connections in Israel. For instance, Tobiah was the son-in-law of Shechaniah, son of Arah. Also, Tobiah's son Johohanan was married to the daughter of Meshullam, son of Berekiah. Tobiah himself had married Shecaniah's daughter. Tobiah also had a daughter-in-law who came from the family of Meshullam, whose name was listed as one of those who made repairs on the wall of Jerusalem in front of their living quarters. So Tobiah was well entrenched into the families and politics of Judah (vv. 18–19). And these relatives made sure Nehemiah kept getting rave reviews of his marvelous person and works. But Nehemiah had reason to think differently: "Tobiah sent letters to intimidate me" (v. 19c). What chutzpah!

Imagine Nehemiah taking a governorship with those kinds of familial and marital ties linking some of your own people to the heart of the opposition. But God was greater than all those possible sources of intimidation as well.

Conclusions

1. Winston Churchill said in the midst of World War II, "Never, give in. Never, never, never, never, never give in."

2. God has given us nine principles for three major challenges to being a leader: for the Challenges of: Intrigue, Innuendo, and Intimidation. But for these challenges there were six divine principles: Discernment, Direction, Directness, Determination, Decisiveness, and a Demonstration of God's Approval.

3. One commentator of old said: "The trouble with God's enemies is not that their knowledge is defective, but their hearts are alienated." The fifty-two days of wall-building were clearly a token of divine assistance, but that evidence did not stop the opposition.

4. Leaders must meditate on the law of God, day and night, if they wish to have good success (Joshua 1:8).

Questions for Discussion and Reflection

1. Is any amount of opposition comparable to the presence and power of the Lord who has called that leader in the first place? Which of the two will fold and be destroyed first?

2. How steady should our hand remain on the work when we are obviously being detracted by other offers to sidetrack us from the major business to which we have been called?

3. Which is harder for a leader to take: external pressure, internal pressure, or attacks on our person?

Lesson 6

Reorganizing the Community
to Help Lead a Revival

Nehemiah 7:1–73b – 8:1–37

Chapter 7 signals that at last "[Nehemiah's] wall had been built and [the] doors [had been set] in place." The initial task to which God had called his servant was now complete. But this did not mean all the problems had been solved, for some issues still reared their heads. But Nehemiah was not a man who let difficulties fester before he dealt with them; instead, as a thoughtful leader, he anticipated where the project of the wall was still vulnerable—even after it was built! According to this leader's analysis, the gap of the times for closing the gates on the wall was the way this whole project might be better managed to secure the city.

So Nehemiah put his brother Hanani in charge of the gates of Jerusalem" (7:1). He felt his brother was "a man of integrity and [one who] feared God more than most men do" (v. 2). And that is the best way to select men to serve along with oneself as a leader. Nehemiah also assigned the "gatekeepers" to manage the city gates, even though they were normally in charge of guarding just the Temple entrance. Nehemiah ordered, "The gates of Jerusalem are not to be opened until the sun is hot" (v. 3). It is also probable that he reinforced these "gatekeepers" with the additional help of the "singers" and "Levites." Some scholars believe "singers" and "Levites" were added to the beginning of the chapter due to a scribal error, transposing text from vv. 43–45, though no evidence supports that supposition. Other scholars incorrectly claim "Hanani" and "Hananiah" were one and the same person, but the phrase in v. 3 is clear: "I said to *them*."

One other uncertainty about the text is in v. 3: Who is speaking? The Hebrew consonantal text reads "and *he* said," but the tradition was "*I* said to them." It's rather difficult to tell, but whoever spoke, whether

Hanani, Nehemiah, or God, it was to ensure the safety of the city and its inhabitants.

This speaker also ordered additional residents of Jerusalem to be employed in the defense of the city, with some appointed to stand guard near their posts and others near their homes (v. 3b). In this way, the security of the city involved the local residents, apparently in a rotating guard-duty (v. 3c)—including people who would have a vested interest in protecting their own homes!

At the time, there were only a few who had chosen to live in the demolished city, as many of the homes were not yet rebuilt from the 586 B.C.E. destruction. Knowing Jerusalem's size, most Israelites had preferred to live in the surrounding villages instead. Nevertheless, God put it on Nehemiah's heart to assemble the nobles, officials, and common people for a general registration of everyone by their families (v. 5). To do this, Nehemiah found the genealogical record of those who had been the first to return home to the land of Israel (v. 5b). This genealogical list in Nehemiah, though similar to the list in Ezra 2, had a different purpose. Nehemiah's purpose was to select those who would live in Jerusalem. Moreover, this census list was approved by God, not motivated by Satan as was the divinely condemned census taken in 1 Chronicles 21:1. In this case, they were the men and women who had returned from the Babylonian exile King Nebuchadnezzar had enforced in his day (v. 6). The list that follows is almost identical to the list found in Ezra 2:1–70, but there are slight differences in some of the names and numbers.[1] This may be due to the recognized difficulty of copying Hebrew numbers.

A good number of commentators on the book of Nehemiah wrestle with the problem of how Nehemiah 7–13 fits into the present context. To be sure, the key reason these chapters were placed here was to emphasize the fact that the covenant with Israel's God had to be renewed, so we are given a series of events that show how that was accomplished.

---

1. H. L. Allrik, "The Lists of Zerubbabel (Nehemiah 7 and Ezra 2) and the Hebrew Numerical Notation," *Bulletin of the American Schools of Oriental Research* Vol. 136 (Dec. 1954): 21–27.

We will not pause to survey or comment on the list of names of the 42,360 returnees, in addition to the 7337 men and maidservants, plus the 245 singers, for the real goal was to get an adequate number to take up residence in Jerusalem. Chapter 7 ends, "When the seventh month came, and the Israelites had settled in their towns…" (v. 73b), while chapter 8 opens with all the returnees gathering "as one man [or "person"] in the square before the water gate" (v. 1). Why all the people suddenly decided to assemble in front of the water gate at this time is not explicitly stated, but it may well have been because on the first of the seventh month, according to Leviticus 23:24, it was celebrated as the beginning of the new year (Rosh Hashanah), originally called the Feast of Trumpets. The seventh month also included the celebration on the tenth day the Day of Atonement (Leviticus 16), and on the fifteenth of the month, the Feast of Tabernacles began, so this was an important time in the spiritual life of the people.

Preparing the Community for a Revival

Nehemiah 8 has three dominant emphases: (1) the "people" occur thirteen times in 8:1–12; (2) the phrase "all the people" occurs nine times; and (3) six times it is recorded that the people's desire was for "discernment" and an "understanding of God's Word" (2, 3, 7, 8, 9, 12). The last item seems to be the central feature of this chapter, if not of the whole revival.

So, let us look at this great chapter on one of Israel's major revivals.

God's Word Will Assuage Their Hunger to Know and Understand It Better – 8:1–8

Good and effective leadership takes the initiative to prompt the people to seek a genuine revival that involves a complete reversal of one's ways and a complete turning of the heart to the Lord. It is rather new, however, to sense that the reading of the law of Moses and the worship of the Living God was not at this time centered in the Temple nor controlled by the priesthood but was under the supervision of Ezra the scribe as authorized by Nehemiah. It would appear, therefore, that from this point forward, the reading and study of the Word of God would take precedence over Temple worship.

The people's desire to understand and discern the meaning of what was being taught in the Bible was altogether appropriate for those who became known as "the people of the Book." The Bible was not designed solely for the priests and the leaders of the nation; rather, it was to be a book for all the people (v. 2). This emphasis on the Word of God became the core of belief from this time well into the early days of the believing community. However, that core began to slip from the center of those professing faith in the community of confessing Jewish and Christian persons, so by the time of the Protestant Reformation, it had to be rediscovered again with the banner of *sola scriptura*.

Note that the people "told Ezra the scribe to bring out the Book of the Law of Moses" (v. 1b). Ezra read aloud from this scroll from "daybreak till noon," so that "all were able to understand it" (v. 2). And "all the people listened attentively to the Book of the Law" (v. 3b). Apparently, an insatiable hunger had built up over the years, and dryness of the soul now demanded that hunger be satisfied by the continual reading of the divine word. The hearing of God's Word, as it was ordained to act, led the people to meet the conditions for revival. The use of these long periods of reading the Word in its extended context brought an end to the famine of hearing the Word of God as the prophet Amos also signified in Amos 8:11, "'The days are coming,' declares the Sovereign LORD, 'when I will send a famine through the land—not a famine of food … but a famine of hearing the words of the LORD.'" That famine of the Word of God precedes and is at the heart of all physical and national famines.

To assist this public reading of God's Word, a large wooden platform had been constructed so all could hear the Word and see the reader as well. Ezra stood in the middle of the platform and was flanked by thirteen lay leaders, six on his left hand and seven on his right. Some think these thirteen men were "priests," though there is no indication that they were either priests or Levites, for a different list of Levities is given later on for those who would help explain the Word of God.

As Ezra opened the Word of God in front of them near the Water Gate, they all instinctively stood up (v. 5) and remained standing for the whole time of the reading of Scripture. The standing of the people was not because of a veneration for the Scripture, but solely because it was the Word of God that was worthy of their praise and adoration. What a great precedent for the congregations today; instead of standing for all of our praise songs of human composition, why not use the principle of standing to honor the Word of God when it is read in public? Our current practice more resembles what is seen at rock concerts than it does a practice that seeks to symbolize theology and give glory to our Lord.

The people responded by lifting their hands in praise to God and saying, "Amen! Amen!" and bowing down their faces to the ground in deep humility (v. 6b–c). Even with such a wonderful reception of the Word, some of the Scriptures still had to be explained (v. 7). The years of captivity must have brought an absence of a knowledge of the Word of God (biblical illiteracy). But the leaders provided, for such gaps in knowledge by using thirteen Levites to instruct the people so the sense of the text became clear to them (v. 7). Some commentators incorrectly assume these Levites translated the text of Scripture from Hebrew into Aramaic, the *lingua franca* of the exiles. But there is no evidence to back up this supposition. Moreover, such an idea does not square with the fact that at the same time period of the post-exilic times, other biblical books were being written in Hebrew, such as Haggai, Zechariah, Malachi, 1 and 2 Chronicles, Ezra, and Nehemiah. The Hebrew word translated as "giving the meaning/sense [of the text]" (v. 8) is hotly debated. Some want to render the Hebrew word to mean "translate" the text, but it does not exhibit that sense until the Targums.

Thus, the Word of God was read, and its meaning was made clear enough that the people could understand what was being read. It is lamentable that a good part of the reason why there is a famine of the Word today is that all too often, those who should proclaim or teach it tend to take a "bumper-sticker approach" in which a phrase, clause or topic from the Bible is adopted from a verse (or part of one), and the context is abandoned or just plain jettisoned. But the entire passage with the details of the pericope is not explained or even mentioned. No wonder the famine grows by the day as we focus on less and less of what God had to say to us.

God's Word Will Become Their Joy and Strength – 8:9–12

Some who comment on the meaning of the text feel that verse 9's "Nehemiah the governor" and "Ezra the priest and scribe" were added by later scribes because the verb "said" in the verse is singular. But others respond that such a construction is common in certain situations. In fact, after Nehemiah had finished building the wall, the people asked Ezra to read from the law of God. Then it was that Nehemiah became active in helping the people to understand what had been read to them (vv. 9, 10).

The entrance of God's Word gave not only light to the soul, but also, as it usually does, brought great joy to the hearts and lives of the people. That is not an unexpected or a novel development, for the most immediate impact a revival can produce is the joy that comes from sins being forgiven. On hearing the Word of God, the audience was convicted very deeply about their sin before God. Take for example these texts from the Pentateuch: Leviticus 26 and Deuteronomy 28. These texts from Moses' law alone, with their warnings about the alternative prospect of either blessing or curse, depending on whether the people trusted the Lord or disobeyed him, would be enough to jar their consciences, The threats of judgment in these texts is so vivid that they must have produced an ominous sense of impending destruction on them if they did not repent and turn from their sin.

In fact, so moved were the people when they heard the Word of the Lord that they began to weep and mourn over their sin (v. 9c). But Nehemiah (perhaps with the help of the Levites in quieting down the people, for the verb "said" is again singular in form) called for a halt to all the weeping and mourning. He instructed all the people, "Go and enjoy choice food and sweet drinks and send some to those who have nothing prepared" (v. 10a). He declared the day to "sacred to the Lord" (v. 10b). They were not to grieve, "for the joy of the LORD [would be their] strength" (v. 10d).

The joy of the Lord comes because we are a forgiven people as well as a people who now have fellowship and communion with a gracious Lord. Also, when God's people know his Word, they are a much happier group of folks to be with (v. 12). Did not the psalmist write, "Great peace have they who love your law, and nothing can make them stumble" (Psalm 119:165). It is sad to see all too many try to bring joy to

God's people by a hundred and one other means, but who fail to feed God's people from the Word of God!

God's Word Will Whet Their Appetites to Learn More – 8:13–18

So moved were the people by hearing God's Word that they not only were reduced to tears and mourning over their sin, but they were intent now on observing every little detail found in the Word (v. 14). Their appetites were so whetted from the second day of the seventh month until the seventh day that they sought out Ezra for more teaching (vv. 13, 18). They learned that the Israelites were to live in booths during the feast of the seventh month (v. 14b; see Ezra 3). They learned that the Feast of Tabernacles or Feast of Booths was to be observed (Leviticus 23:33–43) in that same seventh month. As a result, the folks went out and began cutting down branches on the fifteenth day of the month, including from olive trees, myrtles, and shade trees to fulfill what was written in the law of Moses.

After the people had cut down these branches, they brought them back and built for themselves temporary booths on the flat roofs of their own homes, in the courts of the house of God, as well as in the court of the Water Gate and in the Gate of Ephraim (v. 16). The booth would be a temporary "hut" that would remind them of their days of wandering in the wilderness and living in temporary "lean-tos." This quick assembling of these temporary structures also called to their attention the fact that their lives were, by the very nature of things, very fragile, but their faith in the Lord was far surer, and more abiding, than the structures they lived in! This work involved the entire company that had returned from the Babylonian captivity (v. 17). In fact, not since the days of Joshua, son of Nun, had Israel celebrated anything like they did on this occasion. Their joy knew almost no bounds as the exploded with delight on hearing the Word of God (v. 18).

Ezra continued to read from the Book of the Law of God "day after day" (v. 18) as they celebrated the feast for seven days. On the eighth day, as Scripture taught, there was a sacred assembly.

Conclusions

What an unusual day the people of Judah experienced as Nehemiah, with the aid of the singers, the Levites, and others, directed Ezra the scribe publicly to read the Word of God. What a joy to see what happens when the hunger for God's Word grows so intensely that, when it is read and explained, it results in repentance and downright sorrow for the way we as sinners have been acting in the meantime because of the absence of hearing the Word!

The scandalous behavior of those of us who in our day have confessed Yeshua as our Lord and Savior, has often led to the awful result that a layer of heaviness and a loss of joy and excitement for the things of God lies over the body of believers. This cannot be fixed or resolved until the full use of the Word of God is resumed once again.

May God's people be visited once again with a similar time when our hunger for his Word has reached such a great demand that only the reading and explaining of the Word will once more restore our joy and delight in life and in our walk with God.

Questions for Discussion and Reflection

1. Since God used the long days of captivity in Babylon as the grounds for the people sensing their hunger for his Word, what drastic events currently might have the same effect on us modern believers?

2. In your estimation, what impelled the people to come together at the Water Gate to hear the Word of God? Have you ever witnessed such a time in your lifetime?

3. Many think that there is little or no joy in households of faith today. Do you think the absence of God's Word might be an important missing component of their experience and the absence of joy?

4. Deuteronomy 31:12–13 enjoins the reading of God's Law at the Feast of Tabernacles every seventh year. Can you suggest a similar national day in our culture to make up for this hiatus in our walk as believers?

Lesson 7

Learning from History to Extol the Grace of God

Nehemiah 9:1–38

The prayer of the Levites recorded in Nehemiah 9 is known as the longest prayer in the entire Bible. Moreover, some 22 verses in this prayer come from previous points made by earlier Old Testament writers. And if you add up all the quotations from and allusions to the Word of God in this prayer, there are some 264 references or allusions!

Even though the Levites were the leaders of the worship service, one might best conclude that Ezra himself composed this prayer, for it is very much like the prayer in Ezra 9, which also draws heavily from the theology and history of the people of Israel. The history and theology in this prayer weaves into a single piece the elements of instruction, exhortation, and confession. Understood from that perspective, this prayer was not merely a liturgical or priestly sample; it was also a real prophetic piece at the same time. It seems best to see the author's purpose as showing the close connection that should, and did, exist between reading Scripture, and the people's genuine confession on the day of fasting that came two days after the Feast of Tabernacles. The seven-day Feast was always a time of great joy and rejoicing. But history is more complex than our suppositions as to how it should proceed.

This phenomenon can be illustrated by this event: On January 23, 1996, a minister named Joe Wright from the Central Christian Congregation in Topeka, Kansas, was invited to be a guest chaplain at the Kansas House of Representatives in Wichita. He boldly prayed a prayer of repentance that had been written by Pastor Bob Russell of Southeast Christian Congregation in Louisville, Kentucky. Instead of including the usual politically correct generalities to make the prayer more palatable for this secular audience, his prayer passionately called the American nation to repentance and righteousness—a prayer that is still very relevant in our day as well!

Pastor Wright began the House session by praying in this manner:

Heavenly Father, we come before you today to ask your forgiveness and to seek your direction and guidance. We know what your Word says, "Woe to those who call evil good," but that's exactly what we have done. We have lost our spiritual equilibrium and inverted our values.

We confess that we have ridiculed the absolute truth of your Word and called it moral pluralism. We have worshiped other gods and called it multi-culturalism.

We have endorsed perversion and called it an alternative lifestyle.

We have exploited the poor and called it the lottery.

We have neglected the needy and called it self-preservation.

We have rewarded laziness and called it welfare.

We have killed our unborn children and called it choice.

We have shot abortionists and called it justifiable.

We have neglected to discipline our children and called it building esteem.

We have abused power and called it political savvy.

We have coveted our neighbor's possessions and called it ambition.

We have polluted the air with profanity and pornography and called it freedom of expression.

We have ridiculed the time-honored values of our forefathers and called it enlightenment.

Search us, O God, and know our hearts today; try us and see if there be some wicked way in us; cleanse us from every sin and set us free.

Guide and bless these men and women who have been sent here [to the Kansas state legislature] ... who have been ordained by you to govern this great state. ... May their decisions direct us to the center of your will. I ask it all in the name of your Son, the Living Savior, Jesus Christ. Amen.

At least one legislator walked out in protest during this prayer. However, in the next six weeks, Central Christian Congregation received 6500 calls about the prayer, of which only 47 were negative. The well-known news commentator Paul Harvey ran the story twice on his radio newscast and received the largest response he had ever received to any of his broadcasts.

Clearly this prayer struck a huge responsive note in a wide swath of the American population, for it spoke the truth. It is reported that over the months and years that followed, this prayer was used in Churches in every one of our fitty states. It was indeed a time of national repentance, but it transpired more than two decades ago.

In Nehemiah's day, a similar, strong reaction came from the people of Judah. They too openly confessed their sin before God. It is to this prayer in Nehemiah 9, then, that we now turn our attention.

Introduction: The Setting for Our Confession – 9:1–5

The first reaction of the people to hearing the reading of God's Word was one of sorrow and weeping (8:9). But as it so often happens even today, whenever the Word of God is set forth in all its majesty and power, weeping over our sin is followed by real repentance and confession. The general plan and details of Nehemiah 9:6–37 resemble Psalm 106; however, Nehemiah stops his story of what happened with the congregation's confession, while the psalmist went on to praise God for all he had done.

There was such a strong solidarity of the people of Judah with their ancestors of the past that the congregation confessed not only their own sins, but those of their living relatives and neighbors. This practice is often seen in the Bible and is to be commended even for our own day. For example, in Daniel 9:4–19, Daniel confessed not only his own sins, but in 39 instances he confessed the sins of his forefathers in his prayer as well.

Some think Nehemiah's prayer is too long to have been composed on just one event. They contend that it must have come from several occasions and assembled in chapter 9 as one uninterrupted piece. But just as long psalms were often used in a single offering of prayer, so it is not unreasonable to think the same might have occurred in this case as well.

The people put on "sackcloth" to symbolize their mourning and humility. The reading from the Book of the Law (9:3) made them realize they and their ancestors had constantly failed to observe what Scripture had taught. They had broken their covenant with God. But this departure from our Lord had also created a natural hunger to know God and grow in his Word. This emphasis raised a doublet of challenges: (1) We must allow God to speak through his Word if we wish to be whole again and receive correction, and (2) we must read not only brief devotionals from Scripture, but we must be willing to take the time to hear or read longer sections of Scripture to grasp the context of what is being said. Thus, for Nehemiah's crowd, the first extensive reading of the Word of God took place on the first quarter of the day, as reported in 8:4–8. This was followed by a time of celebration (8:12); the second reading came in 8:14–15, which was followed by the Festival of Tabernacles; and the third reading came in 9:3. It was after this third reading that the crowd followed it with the prayer of confession as they worshiped their Lord.

Recall God's Grace to Us in The Past – 9:6–8

The introductory section of vv. 1–5 ended with the Levites urging all at the Feast of Tabernacles to "stand up and praise the LORD your God, who is from everlasting to everlasting" (9:5b). Perhaps this was a hymn the Levites used as the *introitus* to the prayer of penitence that followed.

This prayer is very similar to such historical psalms as Psalm 78, 105, 106, 135 and 136. In this section of the prayer, they celebrated God's work in the past in creation (v. 6) and in his covenant with Abraham (vv. 7–8).

The hymn to God as Creator (v. 6) is one of exalting the Creator for his work of preservation in creation. The expression "heaven of heavens" is used to express the superlative form in Hebrew; thus, it is at once also a reference to the sun, moon, and stars. Everything in the celestial realm has its life and its existence from God alone. All life comes God; nothing exists on its own merits alone.

Moreover, God has been working for and with the Jewish people for some time now. Accordingly, God chose a man named Abram in the Chaldean town of Ur and brought him out and renamed him Abraham

(v. 7). The fact that God made a covenant with Abraham and the people of Israel is a central feature of the whole Bible. It is this covenant that motivated the people of Israel to obey God's commands, but it was also his covenant that would serve as the basis for his frequent warnings to avoid sin and to prepare for judgment if they strayed from his precepts. A major promise in his list of covenant promises was the land of the Canaanites, which God would give to Israel. The six nations that had previously owned the land of Canaan were mentioned here, from a list of ten that appeared elsewhere (e.g., Genesis 15:19–21), as those whom the Lord had dispossessed their land from their hands and given it to Israel. In fact, so significant is the Hebrew word *natan*, "give," it is used fifteen times in vv. 8–36. Thus, the prayer emphasized all that God had given to his people.

Recall God's Grace in His Past Powerful Deliverances of Us – 9:9–15

As God called the nation of Israel into existence, he made his rescue of the Jews from Egypt the top saving event in their newly developing history. So significant was this single act that some forty words are used to describe the miracles done in Egypt and during the forty years of wandering. This wide vocabulary for the miracles God performed at that time appears some 500 elsewhere in the Old Testament.[1] The one leading in prayer here drew in a large number of parallel passages from other parts of the Old Testament to describe all God had done in redeeming his people.

Verses 11–12 revisit what God had done for Israel in the Exodus (Ex. 13:1–14:30). God had delivered his people from the foreign land of Egypt, just as he later would once again deliver them from Babylon and Persia. But his language does not cease as the Old Testament comes to a close, for the language of deliverance continues to be used of God's liberation of mortals from sin and oppression in this life (Galatians 1:4; 2 Corinthians 1:9–11).

---

1. Mervin Breneman, ed., *The New American Commentary: Ezra, Nehemiah, Esther, v. 10* (Nashville: Broadman & Holman, 1993), 237.

But there were other divine gifts besides deliverances, for vv. 13–15 point to what God did for Israel on Mount Sinai and in the wilderness. God continued to "give" (more of the fifteen times this verb appears in this prayer) to them "laws that are just and right" (v. 13) as well as "bread from heaven" and their thirst for "water from the rock" as he led them to "take possession of the land [he] had sworn with uplifted hand to give them" (v. 15). God's laws were not to be seen as burdens, even his law about the Sabbath. Instead, that law that was contained in the Decalogue pointed out the divine will for men and women. Notice how God's servant Moses still held, at this late date in history, a special place in the estimation of our Lord. No wonder Moses appears in the New Testament eighty-five times (e.g., John 1:15–18; Revelation 15:1–4).

Recall God's Pardoning Grace to Us – 9:16–25

It is clear from the first two words of v. 16 that a mega-change has taken place, for the verse begins with "But they." Instead of Judah recognizing and appreciating all God had done for them, they became "arrogant" and "stiff-necked" as they refused to "obey" all of "God's commands" (v. 16). The "'stiff-necked'-ness" imagery was all too common in everyday life for Judah to miss, for they had often seen that very same stubbornness and resistance in their animals; they would struggle and shake their heads when their owners went to place a yoke on their necks, just as the Jewish people tried to shake off any sort of yoke on their necks.

Amazingly, despite Judah's penchant for acting stubbornly and her refusal to listen or to recall all God's miraculous works on their behalf, even going so far as to "appoint a leader in order to return to their slavery" (v. 17b), the key phrase in this prayer was this: "But you are a forgiving God, gracious and compassionate, slow to anger and abounding in love" (v. 17c). This affirmation began with the expression "But you" (Hebrew *v'attah*), which occurs five times in this prayer (vv. 17, 19, 27, 28, 33). The forgiveness God extended to Judah is the same forgiveness extended to all men, despite how ornery and prone mortals are to resisting his love, favor, and grace. It is a marvel beyond description that after Israel made a calf and announced, "This is [our] god who brought us up out of Egypt" (v. 18), God did not desert Israel, just as he has not deserted us. In his amazing compassion, he refused to abandon Israel in the wilderness (v. 19). Instead, in his faithfulness for those who least deserved it, he led them in the desert by a pillar of cloud by day and a pillar of fire by night (v. 19b). Continually God "gave [his] good Spirit to instruct them" (v. 20a) while he "sustained them in the desert" for forty years, so that "they lacked nothing; their clothes did not wear out nor did their feet become swollen" (v. 21).

Tragically, Israel received the gift of the land of Canaan without acknowledging that kingdoms and nations had been transferred to them by the hand of God (v. 22a). This was happening all the while as the Lord "made their sons as numerous as the stars in the sky" (v. 23)—a reference to the promise God had anciently given to Abraham (see Genesis 12:2, 15:5). God "subdued before them the Canaanites, who lived in the land" as he "handed the Canaanites over to them, along with their kings and the peoples of the land" (v. 24b–c). Instead of destroying the conquered cities (except Jericho, Ai and Hazor, which they burnt down), they merely "took possession of [their enemy's] houses ... wells ... vineyards, olive groves, and fruit trees in abundance" (v. 25c). In summary, "They ate to the full and were well nourished; they reveled in [God's] great goodness" (v. 25d).

Recall God's Gracious Training of Us – 9:26–37

In spite of all of God's goodness to Israel, the prayer continued to acknowledge an old familiar pattern of backsliding in the nation of Israel, which had appeared with regularity in Judges: (1) disobedience to the law of God led to (2) the divine handing over of the nation to their enemies. Then the people would (3) cry out for God's rescue of them, to which God (4) answered by delivering them from the crisis they had fallen into as a result of their sin. One would think they, and we, would learn our lesson and trust and serve God with all our hearts and souls. Yet, this pattern took place time after time. God would abandon them (v. 26b) and leave them in the hands of their enemies until misery found a voice that acknowledged the depths to which they had fallen.

But the people never learned the lesson. "They sinned against your ordinances, by which a man will live if he obeys them" (v. 29b; Leviticus 18:5; Deuteronomy 4:1, 30:16; Galatians 3:12). This was not an alternative path to salvation; it argued that if a man heeded what God had commanded, he would "live in the sphere of them" (Greek locative idea).

This stubborn rebellion to walking in the instruction of God's Word went on year after year even though Israel was admonished by the prophets God sent to them (v. 30). Yet even though Israel paid no attention to what God commanded, but instead turned their backs on him, the Lord still "in [his] great mercy did not put an end to them or abandon them, for [he is] a gracious and merciful God" (v. 31).

The Levites boldly prayed that "the great, mighty, and awesome God, who keeps his covenant of love," not let the "hardship that had come upon Judah "seem to be trifling in [his] eyes" (v. 32). They agreed God had been "just" and "acted faithfully" in all the trouble that had come on them from Assyria, Babylon, and Persia, while they together had done "wrong" (v. 33). Neither Judah's "kings, leaders, priests, or fathers" had paid any attention to all God had commanded or what he had warned would happen if they abandoned him (v. 34). It is astounding that all the time they were in the "spacious and fertile" land of Canaan and had enjoyed all God's "goodness," "they did not serve [him] or turn from their evil ways" (v. 35b).

That would explain the position the Jewish nation was in at that time: they were "slaves" (v. 36a). The Persians ruled over their "bodies" and "their cattle" just as they pleased; "[They were] in great distress" (v. 37b).

Because of this state of affairs, the Levites were going to make a binding agreement with God and the people (v. 38a).

Conclusions

This prayer began as a result of the people's decision to fast and dress in sackcloth for all the sins they and their forebearers had accumulated.

Questions for Discussion and Reflection

How is this ninth chapter of Nehemiah related to the eighth chapter? What does this tell us about the fruit of revival and its effects?

Lesson 8

Leaders Who Signed
a Binding Agreement

Nehemiah 9:38–10:39

Even though some say Nehemiah 10:1–13:31 does not belong in the book, 9:38 sees it differently, beginning, "In view of all this," meaning all that had been written in chapters 1–8. The author of Nehemiah saw this important "agreement" made by the people as their wonderful response to the revival called for in chapter 8, and to Ezra's prayer in chapter 9, which formed the next step in the whole string of events the nation was encountering. Since a genuine and encouraging revival followed the people's hearing and responding to God's Word, it turned into a confession of sin for which Ezra prayed on their behalf. The author of this book went on to tell how the people reacted after they heard the declaration of God's law read from the Torah and therefore committed themselves to obey God.

The Hebrew word *karat*, "to cut" or "to make a covenant" (Hebrew *b'rit*) is the word often used in the Old Testament for "making [or literally "cutting"] a covenant." In this chapter, though, the verb "to cut" is used uniquely with the word *amana*, "agreement." Why the author of Nehemiah chose that word instead of a "covenant" (*b'rit*) is not known, but Mervin Breneman[1] suggests it may have been because Ezra had just recalled in his prayer that Abraham used the root of the same word *'aman* ("to believe") in God's covenant, thus a word from the same root must have been on his mind (Genesis 15:6). That would be a natural link, then, between the two texts!

The leaders, Levites and priests made a "binding agreement," "put [it] into writing" and "affixed their seals to it." The community was now on record that they would live just as the Word of God taught. The

---

1. Mervin Breneman, *Ezra, Nehemiah, Esther*, 243.

"seal," of course, was a sign that these people were now giving their legal consent to this document. God's Word would now be the statute and the principle by which they would live as a community and as the people of God. The first one to sign the "agreement" was none other than Nehemiah the governor. This is the only place in the Old Testament where the word "agreement" is used as an alternative word for "covenant."

The Priests, Levites and Leaders Who Signed the Document – 10:1–27

The written document had the signatures of the leaders of the people attached to it as a means of placing on it a "seal." First came the names of 21 priests, after priority had been given to the names of Nehemiah and to Zedekiah (vv. 2–8). Ezra's name does not appear, but this is likely because Ezra belonged to the family of Seriah, as did the high priest Eliashib. Of the 21 names, 15 are the names of families.

There were 17 Levites who signed the document (vv. 9–12). Some of the names may have been family names rather than personal names. Some are the same names as those who returned with Zerubbabel in 12:8, and seven names are those who also had taught the people God's law in 8:7.

The names of other leaders of the people who signed the document (vv. 14–27) were mostly family names. The first 21 names in vv. 14–20a parallel rather closely the list in Ezra 2:3–30 and Nehemiah 7. The other 23 names refer to some families who helped build the wall.

The Oath to Separate Themselves –10:28–29

It was necessary for the leaders of the community to publicly sign the agreement, for it became the basis for the actions that followed from the rest of the people. Thus, the leaders led by showing the people the way they too should go. The biblical doctrine of "separation" from the secular world, or its culture, is unfortunately not mentioned today as much as it used to be in many independent and Baptistic churches. But as Brenenman notes:

> Separation from the neighboring peoples was important to maintain the distinctive beliefs and ethical principles of the community. God still wants his people to be separate by repudiating the values and beliefs that are contrary to his will. We must take seriously the Scriptural emphasis on separation without falling into an isolationist situation. [On the other hand], the other danger is to accommodate the world so much that we fall into a syncretism that loses our Christian way of thinking and acting. In the situation of Ezra and Nehemiah, separation was imperative to secure the continuity of the redeemed community.[2]

It is noteworthy that "sons/brothers and daughters" were included as persons of particular significance. All too often the older generation neglects the younger part of the community, and therefore they do not build carefully for the future.

This agreement of the leaders and the people involved, as all covenants did, a "curse," as well as an oath of support. For example, God's covenant with Israel in Moses' day was offered with both curses and blessings (Deuteronomy 27:15–26, 30:19). This is why the people clearly understood that when an oath was broken in their covenants, one could expect a curse would occur. The expected judgment was meant to keep the community walking in the paths of obedience. Only when the whole community submitted to the authority and ongoing relevance of the Word of God were they freed from the otherwise-expected judgments from heaven.

Examples of the Expected Secular Separation – 10:30–39

In order to show the sincerity and willingness of the people to heed the injunction to be separate from all compromises with the Word of God, the congregation promised not to give their daughters in marriage to the pagan peoples living around them (v. 30). This warning, along with other examples in vv. 30–39, was based on the laws recorded in the Torah of Moses, but in this instance, they were applied to current and specific situations. Some see this process as the very beginnings of

---

2. Marvin Brenenman, *Ezra, Nehemiah, Esther*, 246.

scriptural exegesis, which later in Jewish thought developed into the Jewish Mishna and Talmud.[3]

Another example was observance of the Sabbath day and year, which too had its origins in the Torah. But here again there were new cases that explained the further use of this law, which separated the Jewish people from those they were living among. The Jews were intermingled with neighbors who did not follow the Lord or his commands, so the opportunity to buy and sell on the Sabbath was all too tempting. This called for another decision in which they had to separate themselves from the culture. Likewise, the decision about the Sabbatical seventh year called for combining older laws to new situations in yet another test of the laws of Torah. Exodus 23:10–11 taught that the land was to rest every seventh year from growing any planted seed, and 21:2–6 taught that debt-slaves, who were working off their debts, were to have their debts canceled every seventh year and they were to go free at the end of that time (Deuteronomy 15:1–2).

Every time a Believer is confronted with biblical laws such as these, the question arises as to how relevant are they for our modern observance? Our answer is that only the *principles* embodied in these civil laws are for our obedience today. For example, we are to observe the principle of setting aside one day of each week to worship the Lord and rest, On the other hand, we do not have anything today such as the seventh-Sabbatical year for those who are farming, but the wise farmer takes the principle seriously as he periodically designates part of his farmland to be taken out of production for a full year and places on it a green cover crop that can be plowed under at the end of that growing season to improve the fertility of the soil.

Nehemiah 10:32-33 and Nehemiah 13:10 referred to a new law that had not appeared previously: the Temple tax. Now that the Persian economy had introduced the beginnings of a cash-based economy, for what had previously been one that involved only animals and agricultural actual products as the medium of exchange, but now such a transaction involved the exchange of money (cf. Exod. 30:11-16; 38:25-

---

3. I am indebted to Marvin Brenenman, p. 247, n. 48 for his reference to D. J. A. Clines, "Nehemiah 10 as an Example of Early Jewish Biblical Exegesis," *JSOT* 6.21 (Oct. 1981): 111–17.

26). Moreover, this responsibility of the people for the Temple tax now listed the various uses this money could be put to: (1) The purchase of the bread on the Shewbread table (Lev. 24:6), (2) The purchase of the regular grain offerings and burnt offerings (Exod. 29:38-42; Num. 28:3-8), (3) The gift of offerings made on the Sabbath, New Moon, and feasts, (Num. 28:9-29: 30), as well as (4) holy Offerings, (5) sin Offerings (Lev. 4:1-5; Num. 15:22-29), (6) and all duties in the house of God for its upkeep and cleaning.

In addition to all of these, there were offerings of other kinds included in this list by which the people were to show their careful acts of separation (vv. 34–39). There were set times, appointed by lot, when the people were to bring to the house of God a contribution of wood (v. 34). Then there were gifts each year of the offering of "Firstfruits" (vv. 35–36). Leviticus 6:12–13 had stipulated that the fire of the altar was to be kept burning at all times.

Conclusion

Chapter 10 concludes with ensuring there were storage rooms provided for storing up the gifts from the community, which consisting of ground meal, fruit, wine, and oil. The Levites were to collect the tithes in each town where they worked (v. 37).

This chapter contains many details that the community of the day was to observe. However, there are just as many challenges for the Believer in our day from this same chapter. First among these is the constant need to submit to the authority and power of the Word of God. Believers must also be more mindful of their partnership in the community and fellowship of those who trust in the coming Messiah. Therefore, they need to hold firmly to their word of agreement to the doctrines and goals of the believing community. There is also the need to be wholly given over to the Lord. Often this will mean taking a stand to be separate from the values and practices of the unbelieving persons among whom they live. Finally, it will mean a record of faithfulness in our attendance at the house of God and faithfully storing up in God's house the gifts, offerings and tithes set aside to allow the work of God to prosper.

Questions for Discussion and Reflection

1. How would you define the biblical practice or doctrine of "separation from the culture"? How would you suggest a person avoid being a total isolationist on one hand but also one who accommodates himself fully to the culture of his own day?

2. How useful do you think the signing and sealing of an agreement is to the health of the community or to the status of your own testimony?

3. Do "curses" have any meaning or impact on our lives today? Or in these New Testament times, are only blessings part of what we inherit?

4. How important is it to marry only those who are fellow believers? What should a person do if they come to believe in the Lord after they have been married to an unbeliever?

Leaders Dedicate the Wall And Call for Reform

Nehemiah 11:1–13:31

Thus far, the book of Nehemiah has followed a fairly clear pattern of events that involved (1) the construction of the walls, chapters 1–6; (2) the spiritual revival that followed, chapters 8–10; and (3) the organization and reformation of the community, chapters 11–13. Nehemiah has graciously focused on the "people" rather than on himself, or other important individuals, which shows he was certainly a humble, servant-type leader.

But now that the wall was completed and the safety of the people in the holy city of Jerusalem and its inhabitants had been secured, suddenly it became clear there were not enough people living in Jerusalem to maintain the kind of constant security that was intended for the city. Of course, the "leaders of the people" had "settled in Jerusalem" already (11:1), but that number was insufficient for the goals Nehemiah aspired to for its defense. So to make up for this deficiency, "the rest of the people cast lots to bring one out of every ten [of the returnees], who were living in the towns outside of Jerusalem, to live in Jerusalem, the holy city, while the remaining nine were to stay in their own towns" and villages (v. 1b). In addition to those chosen by lots, there were others who already had graciously volunteered to take up residence in Jerusalem.

It is instructive to again see how prominent the "leaders" were in this book. Here is a model for an effective organization involved in the work of God: (1) There must be leaders who know how to lead and who will lead, and (2) there must be followers who will volunteer, or who will fill the assignments laid out for them, as chosen by lots or by other means!

It may give some contemporary believers pause when they see the community relying on the use of "lots," as if this were all a matter of random chance! But our Lord can use different means to make his will and desires known. In this case, he used the method of lots (which were under his guidance and direction) to guide the believing community. This divine usage of lots can be seen in other passages: (1) to determine which tribe would inherit which part or plot of land in the Promised Land (Numbers 26:55–56); (2) in the impartial division of the dates that Aaron's sons were assigned to minister in the sanctuary of God (1 Chronicles 24:1–5); (3) in designating those who were to minister in the sanctuary as "singers," or who would play the harp, cymbals and lyres (1 Chronicles 25:1–8); and (4) in choosing Matthias to replace Judas as one of the Apostles (Acts 1:23–26).

Jerusalem is referred to as "the holy city" (1), a title rarely found elsewhere in the Old Testament (Isaiah 48:2, 53:1; Daniel 9:24). Because Jerusalem was set apart to the Lord from the rest of the cities of the world, it was entitled to be known as "the holy city."

Those Who Moved to Jerusalem – 11:3–24

In these verses we have another of the many lists in Ezra-Nehemiah. Those mentioned here include priests, Levites, and Temple ministers, especially those who came from Judah and Benjamin (vv. 3–9). All these were people who had lived in other towns and villages. Apparently, these lists were by no means complete: 1 Chronicles 9 includes many more names, along with names of those from other tribes besides Judah, Benjamin, and Levi. These men were also called "able men" (Hebrew *'anshe hayil*), as well as later in v. 14, where the NIV again translates it as "able men," though here the Hebrew is *gibbore hayil*, a term used of military men, which could also be rendered "mighty men of valor." Presumably they were part of military personnel who were to be used in defending the Temple area. One group at the end of v. 14 is called *haggedolim*, possibly meaning "the great ones." Others rendered it as "a leading family." Verse 16b refers to those "who had charge of the outside work of the house of God," which points to the fact that there were different types of work assigned to the Levites, such as gathering and storing up what was needed for the care and provisions of the Temple building and associated venues.

Another title that arrests our attention is "the director who led in thanksgiving and prayer" (v. 17). It is fascinating to find all the way back in that time that the one who directed the worship of God was significant enough to be specially singled out as important. This calls us to pay attention to those who shape and form the so-called "praise teams" in our contemporary services, for they carry a great responsibility in shaping the values and theology of leading God's people in worship. These tasks ought to be given prayerful and Spirit-guided consideration, even in our own day, lest we regard that part of the service that precedes the preaching as merely part of "the preliminaries"—a poor view of that part of worship!

The list of gatekeepers in v. 19 are not said in this context to be Levites, but they are so designated in 1 Chronicles 9:23–26, 26:1–19, where their duties are also specified. V. 21 refers to the *netinim*, "Temple servants," who were not included in the list in vv. 3–20, because they apparently already lived in Jerusalem. They lived in "the Hill of Ophel," at the north end of the city, just south of the Temple platform area (v. 21). Moreover, "the singers were responsible for the services at the house of God" and "were under the king's orders" (vv. 22–23). But does the word "king" here refer to the Persian king, just as previously these singers were said to be under the supervision of another king—King David? Verse 24 seems to confirm this idea.

It is difficult to know how to place the towns listed in vv. 25–36. Obviously, the list includes towns far to the south in the Negev, where there must have lived some Jewish peoples mixed in with the Gentile population. It did include cities from the old area of the tribe of Benjamin. This list is also similar to the list in Joshua 15, so the mystery remains.

The Repopulation of the Holy City – 11:1–24

It seems the leaders took the lead in making Jerusalem their residence (v. 1a) even before they cast lots to fill the remaining vacuum of needed residents in the Holy City (vv. 1b–2). Once again, the book of Nehemiah demonstrates a beautiful balance between effective leadership and an obedient dependence on God's instructions. These two principles do not need to conflict with each other, nor should they be opposed to each other. The decision was to assign ten percent of the people living in the outlying towns and villages to complete the required number of residents needed to reside in Jerusalem. When some of the people "volunteered to live in Jerusalem," the "people commended" all who "volunteered" (v. 2b). This shows there was a good spirit of cooperation and kindness that indicated the good spiritual health and vitality of the community.

Not all those who had tasks in the Temple lived in Jerusalem, but they "lived in the towns of Judah" (v. 3). Verses 4–24 give us another list for which Ezra-Nehemiah are so rich in content, yet even these lists apparently were incomplete, as parallel lists in 1 Chronicles 9 would seem to indicate. But there is no reason to doubt they were authentic lists—at least for those that were available up to that time. The list included those who were descended from Judah (vv. 4b–6), who the NIV labeled as "able men" (Hebrew, *'anshe hayil*), which could just as well be rendered "men of wealth/substance" or even "valiant/brave men." There is not enough context to decide which concept is operative here, but the writer of Scripture wanted to make sure we understood they were distinguished for some very good reason.

There is also a list in vv. 10–14 of the priests who moved to Jerusalem. In v. 14 the NIV again says they were "able men," but this time the writer used a stronger term, *gibbore hayil*, which could be rendered more militaristically as "mighty men of valor/bravery." Verse 14 ends by noting that the "chief officer" of this list of priests in vv. 10–14 was "Zabdiel, son of Haggedolim," whose final name may not be a personal name, but when translated literally, meant one who belonged to "the great ones." Moreover, the total number of priests in the 1 Chronicles 9:13 list totals 1760 persons, but here in Nehemiah 11:10–14, the total is 1192 (822 + 242 + 128)!

In addition to the lists of lay families in vv. 3–9, and the priests in vv. 10–14, vv. 15–24 gives us one other list—the Levites and gatekeepers in Jerusalem. This list especially notes those who did "the outside work of the house of God" (v. 16), which must have involved both gathering the material needed for the upkeep of the house of God as well as the care, maintenance and preservation of the building and property. This list also notes that "Mattaniah son of Mica, son of Zabdi, the son of Asaph, [was] the director who led in thanksgiving and prayer" (v. 17). Such responsibility again called for special recognition in light of the importance given to the quality of worship in the community. The gatekeepers who are registered here are not said to be Levites, though they are so designated in 1 Chronicles 9:23–26; 26:1-19, as already noted.

We wonder why the "Temple servants" in vv. 21–22, who were also called in Hebrew *netinim*, were not part of the original list in vv. 3–20. The answer seems to be that they already were living in Jerusalem on the "Hill of Ophel," located, as noted, on the north end of the city, just south of the Temple platform area.

The "singers" "were under the king's orders," just as they had been responsible in King David's day (1 Chronicles 25). The question here, though, is what "king" is this text referring to? Some, for good reasons, suggest it is the Persian king! This interpretation seems to be confirmed by v. 24, which talks about "Pethahiah," "who was the king's agent in all affairs relating to the people." This was the Persian king's official advisor, to whom he turned for advice on affairs relating to the Jewish people.

Other Judean Cities Populated at the Time – 11:25–36

A list is given of those who lived in other cities in Judah and Benjamin at this time. The problem with this list is it seems somewhat similar to the list in Joshua 15. This may be because of the extent and shape of the land Judah may have taken at various times. Some of the towns mentioned appear to be outside of Judah, such as Ono and those towns/villages located in the Negev. This list may also have included towns that had a mixed Jewish presence along with other nationalities.

Earlier Lists of Returning Priests and Levites – 12:1–26

Chapter 12 starts with more lists of priests and Levites who were part of the first group to return to Judah from Babylon under Governor Zerubbabel (vv. 1–11). But in vv. 12–21 are names of priests who came back in the time of King Jehoiakim, which were part of the second generation of returnees, followed by lists that add further details to the records (vv. 22–26).

First came the list of priests who came back in the first return from exile under Zerubbabel's leadership (vv. 1–7). This was followed by a list of Levites who also came back under Governor Zerubbabel (vv. 8–9). Mattaniah's family was once again mentioned as being in charge of "the songs of thanksgiving" (v. 8; see 11:17, 12:25).

Next was a list of High Priests (vv. 10–11), beginning with *Jeshua*, or "Joshua," whom we know from the books of Haggai and Zechariah. Eliashib was the High Priest during the time of Nehemiah (v. 10), who was preceded by "Joiakim" as High Priest before Nehemiah's time. That would make him High Priest in Ezra's time. Many of these names appear in Elephantine Letters and in Josephus' history as well.

The Elephantine Letters mention a High Priest known as Johanan (410 B.C.E.), which has concerned some commentators about the reliability of these lists. However, it was customary to use the identical names over and over in alternating generations, so the Josephus reference to Jaddua as High Priest at the time of the fall of the Persian Empire (331 B.C.E.) means Josephus' list may be from a later generation, repeating an identical name.

The lists of priests in vv. 12–21 is similar to the list in 10:2–8, but it is expanded to include six more names.

Finally, vv. 22–26 include more data on the Levites, but once again this list raises questions about chronicles and genealogy. Verse 22 points to the same situation we faced in vv. 10–11. It concerns Johanan, who is best understood as the brother of Joida, whom he followed as High Priest. In v. 23, Kidner says, Johanan is best described as the "son of" Eliashib.[1] The Elephantine Letters relate that Johanan was High Priest in

---

1. Derek Kidner, *Ezra and Nehemiah* (Downers Grove, IL: InterVarsity, 1979), 144.

410 B.C.E., as noted, in the reign of Darius II. Verse 22 called him "Darius the Persian" to distinguish Darius I from Darius the Mede, who also appears in Daniel.

Verse 25 places the verse divider in the wrong spot, removing "Mattaniah, Bakbukiah, [and] Obadiah" from the list of singers in v. 24, but per 11:17, they belong to that list. The other three men in v. 25 are gatekeepers. In v. 24, the named Levites "stood opposite them to give praises and thanksgiving; one section responding antiphonally to the other, as prescribed by David the man of God." This refers to the practice of antiphonal singing that David seems to have introduced to Israel, in which two choirs were used to answer each other with different parts of the song as they were rendering it in worship. David is uniquely called the "man of God" (12:36; 2 Chronicles 8:14). Normally "a man of God" meant "prophet," and while he does qualify as a prophet, here in v. 24 it pointed to the fact that as a man, like Moses, he founded the worship of God.

Verse 26 refers to "the days of Nehemiah the governor and Ezra the priest and scribe." This has raised a debate over whether these two men were contemporaries for any part of their lives, an association most scholars seem to reject. But the two are mentioned as sharing some portion of time together, even though the stretch of time is admittedly very long. The fact that the book of Ezra does not mention Nehemiah even once is not in itself all that unusual, for two other contemporaries, Haggai, and Zechariah, also do not mention each other in their two books, even though they are both ministering at the same time. Why that is so, I do not know!

The Dedication of the Wall – 12:27–47

Now that the wall was completed, it was time for a glorious celebration. Levites and singers were sought out from the places where they lived and brought together to "celebrate joyfully" with "songs of thanksgiving and the music of cymbals, harps, and lyres" (v. 27). After the Levites and singers had been purified ceremonially, "they purified the people, the gates and the wall" (v. 30b). The text does not say how long after the wall's completion this celebration took place, but whenever it was, there was plenty of rejoicing and thanksgiving to God, just as the law required (Deuteronomy 12:7, 12, 18). With the wall completed, Cyrus' decree was fulfilled (Ezra 1:1–5). This was nothing less than the work of God, and it had been beautiful to witness.

Nehemiah did not put himself forward as the man who had suggested this project to King Artaxerxes, or as the one who had successfully led the project. Instead, we find him putting forth "the leaders of Judah" to "go up on top of the wall" as part of two large choirs, whom he would send in opposite directions around the entire wall to meet halfway around as a key part in the dedication ceremony (v. 31).

The choir that went to the right was led by "Hoshaiah," along with "half the leaders of Judah," accompanied by some priests with trumpets and other musical instruments (vv. 32, 36). Ezra the scribe led this procession past the Dung Gate, past the house of David, to the Water Gate on the east side (vv. 31, 37).

The second choir went in the opposite direction, with Nehemiah following! (v. 38) This choir went past the Tower of the Ovens, over the Gate of Ephraim, the Jeshanah Gate, the Fish Gate, the Tower of Hananel and the Tower of Hundred to the Sheep Gate as they stopped at the Gate of the Guard (vv. 38–39).

For those who have visited Jerusalem, as I have, and have walked around the wall of Jerusalem, there is one psalm that quickly comes to mind, as it did when I first toured around the wall: Psalm 48:12–14…

> Walk about Zion, go around her,
> Count her towers,
> Consider well her ramparts,
> View her citadels,
> That you may tell of them
> to the next generation.
> For this God is our God for ever and ever.
> He will be our guide even to the end.

At the same time, Nehemiah appointed men to be in charge of the storerooms, where the "firstfruits and tithes" from the contributions of the people were to be stored (v. 44). The priests and Levites "pleased" the Lord, for their teachings came from the Word of God and not just what they felt what the congregation would accept. Their appeal was to what was taught long ago in the "days of David and Asaph"; thus, theirs were "songs of praise and thanksgiving to God" (v. 46). In summary, then, "in the days of Zerubbabel and Nehemiah, all Israel contributed the daily portions for the singers and the gatekeepers" (v. 47). The people of Judah also "set aside the portion God had directed them to give to the other Levites, as the Levites set aside the portion designated for the descendants of Aaron" (v. 47b).

Further Reforms of Nehemiah – 13:1–31

Even after Judah had earlier experienced a revival (chapter 8), there were continuous needs for teaching on needed reforms and changes in the lifestyle of the people. In this sense, chapter 13 is almost anticlimactic after the wall has been built and those who were already dedicated to the Lord in the community. But the integrity of their lives still had to accord with what was taught in Scripture, so the teaching on reform was needed on a continuing basis for the people in that day and ours.

Separation from Unbelievers – 13:1–3

The text does not indicate that it was a special day when the Book of Moses was read aloud "in the hearing of the people" (v. 1). But the reading of this word taught, "No Ammonite or Moabite or any descendants may enter the assembly of the LORD, even down to the tenth generation" (v. 1b). This was a quotation from Deuteronomy 23:3–6, where some reasons were also given for such a strong word of judgment from God. First of all, the Ammonites had failed to meet the Israelites with any bread or water as they approached their borders. The Moabites went so far as to hire a Gentile foreigner, a so-called prophet named Balaam, to pronounce a curse on Israel. But such a request to curse Israel was impossible, for God had already blessed them instead (Numbers 22:3–11, see Genesis 12:3). The lack of hospitality from these descendants of Lot was seen as an offense against them, even to the "tenth [future] generation." The word "ten" may indicate "completeness" or possibly "forever," as it does in other parts of Scripture. To be sure, every soul was responsible for his or her own sin (Deuteronomy 24:16), but there were instances where the decisions of some groups of people or generations can and did impact the lives of their children, grandchildren and even on into future generations!

The judgments described here were not racially motivated, but they called for a separation from the culture based on doctrinal purity and the call for the exercise of faith. Moreover, in the same context, Israel is warned in Deuteronomy 23:7–8 "not to abhor an Edomite, for he is your brother." Neither were they allowed "to abhor an Egyptian, because [Israel] lived as an alien in [their] country." In fact, Deuteronomy 23:8 continued by teaching: "The third generation of children born to these Edomites, and Egyptians may enter the assembly of the LORD," so grace was greater that sin of any people! Thus, in this instance, we see that the provisions of grace were available even to the foreigner!

Separation of Uncleanliness – 13:4–9

Eliashib the priest was closely associated with Tobiah by marriage but was also an Ammonite. Therefore, this Tobiah, who is also mentioned in 6:10 as being married to a Jew and was one of the key agitators who opposed Nehemiah's reforms, was a *persona non grata* in Judah. It was a matter of great concern, therefore, when Nehemiah discovered Tobiah had been given a large room in the Temple storerooms, which had previously been used to store grain offerings, incense, and Temple articles, and the tithes of new grain, new wine, and oil for the Levites. Instead of being used as designated, it was now being set aside for Tobiah's own personal use! (v. 8) Surely Eliashib knew about Tobiah's earlier opposition to Nehemiah, so why did he now permit it? Was it because Nehemiah had left to return to the Persian king? Such permission by Eliashib gave Tobiah a platform of influence in the community. Nehemiah was not going to allow this action! His absence had provided for all sorts of abuses and sinful practices, which had to be dealt with immediately. Nehemiah had served as governor for twelve years (445–433 B.C.E.), and then he had returned to serve King

Artaxerxes. Later (we do not know exactly when) Nehemiah returned to Jerusalem, apparently to the surprise of the new community in Judah and took swift action. And when he did, he set to work on enacting real reform.

Had Nehemiah not already mentored faithful leaders who could continue the work he had begun? Or were the forces of opposition just too strong for those he trained and left in charge? It is clear he regarded what Eliashib had done as an "evil thing" (v. 7). Nehemiah took charge and immediately began throwing all of Tobiah's personal goods out of the occupied storeroom in the house of God (v. 8). Nehemiah ordered that the rooms Tobiah had occupied were to be purified and the original equipment restored as they had been intended to be used in the Temple (v. 9), for Eliashib had compromised the use of God's house with some of the very people who had so violently opposed the restoration of the walls of Jerusalem.

Separation from Laxity of Observance of Spiritual Things – 13:10–14

Perhaps Nehemiah learned of more abuse and outright moral laxity of what God had instructed the people to do as he cleaned out the storerooms occupied by Tobiah (12:47, 13:10). What had been assigned to the Levites and singers as the storage space for their portions out of the tithe and related gifts in the house of God, had been commandeered for non-scriptural bases. The servants of the house of God "had gone back to their own fields," which they needed to do of necessity if they were to exist (v. 10b). Now we can see how the spiritual demise of the leaders had begun to affect the spiritual life of the servants of God and the people as well.

To Nehemiah, that the Levites and singers had been so badly neglected was nothing less than evidence that God and the things belonging to him had been severely neglected. Moses had instructed Israel long ago that the people's tithes were to support the Levites (Numbers 18:21; see Neh. 9:38–10:39). When Nehemiah first challenged the people to tithe for this purpose, they gave "joyfully"

(12:44). Now what was needed was a strong leader who would restore the habit of giving and help the folks overcome their greed and laxity. Nehemiah put Shelemiah the priest, Zadok the scribe, and a Levite named Pedaiah in charge of the storerooms. He also made Hanan their assistant for distributing the supplies to their brothers.

Separating the Sabbath from the Other Days of the Week – 13:15–22

Among the abuses Nehemiah found was Judah's disregard for the Sabbath. It had become common for men in Judah to tread their winepresses on the Sabbath and bring in their grain and load it on their donkeys, along with wine, grapes, figs, and all sorts of other tasks. Nehemiah ordered that these practices had to stop (15c). Among those desecrating the Sabbath were men from the city of Tyre, who often stayed overnight in Jerusalem. These men brought in fish along with other types of merchandise and sold them on the Sabbath to the people of Judah (v. 16). Nehemiah boldly rebuked the nobles of Judah, telling them that by allowing this, they were doing a very "wicked thing" (v. 17). This leader reminded the nobles that it was precisely why they had been exiled before, for seventy years; thus, they were once again setting themselves up for God's wrath (v. 18).

To halt these sinful practices, Nehemiah ordered the city gates be closed for the Sabbath as soon as the evening shadows appeared the previous evening (v. 19). To make sure this was done, Nehemiah posted some of his own men at the gates (v. 19c). After this, on one or two occasions some of the merchants and sellers of such goods camped outside of Jerusalem's walls overnight, but again Nehemiah warned them that if they did so again, he would lay his hands on them. That took care of the situation (v. 21).

Resting on the Sabbath was very important in the Tenach (Old Testament); the topic is raised frequently (Genesis 2:2; Exodus 16:23–29, 20:8–11, 31:14–16, 35:2–3; Numbers 15:32–36; Amos 8:5; Isaiah 58:13–14; Jeremiah 17:19–27). To choose to disregard the Sabbath was a sure sign that other areas of God's will were being neglected just as brazenly and defiantly.

The principle of observing one day in seven is still, in principle, the norm for believers, even though Believers do not continue to do so on the seventh day. A strong reason for this change is that rather that marking off this day of remembrance of God's resting on the seventh day in creation, or of Israel's deliverance from Egypt, it now marks the day Yeshua rose again from the dead! The Old Testament law hinted at this when it often required Israel to observe not only the seventh day as part of the festival days in which they were to do no work or labor, but they were often required to regard the *eighth day* among their festivals and appointed feasts (e.g., "the day after the Sabbath" [the eighth day] also is "a day of rest" (Leviticus 23:15, 23, 35, 39). Thus, the early congregation met on the first day of the week as best their schedules allowed them to!

Separation Restored – 13:23–31

Earlier, both Ezra and Nehemiah had strongly opposed mixed marriages (Ezra 9–10; Neh. 6:18, 10:30). Now again, as he returned to Jerusalem, he caught men who had married women from Ashdod, Ammon, and Moab (v. 23). The problem wasn't xenophobia or racism; it was a matter of his being pure in heart. Such laxity would threaten family relationships and the theology of the future generations if Judah made no provisions for tithing a part of their time to worship God. So serious was this breach of God's Word that Nehemiah took direct action against those who had married foreign wives (v. 25). But note carefully, what is condemned here is not intermarriage between the races, or some type of racial superiority, but intermarriage with unbelievers! It was being unequally yoked in marriage.

So prevalent were some of these abuses that even the family of the High Priest had fallen into this type of sin. Did not King Solomon get the country into trouble by his sinning in this manner? (v. 26)

Thus, Nehemiah purified the priests and Levites from everything foreign (v. 30). He was bound and determined that under God the people of Judah would not tolerate evil and fall back into a lackadaisical attitude. If the effects of revival were to remain, reformation must follow it to conserve its benefits.

Conclusions

1. The "lot" belongs to the Lord, for even decisions that appear to be arbitrary are in the lap of the Lord (Proverbs 16:33). Nothing is viewed to biblical terms as being merely an accident or the result of luck or chance. Should believers leave anything to chance, or should they even participate in games of chance?

2. Singing was a real and necessary part of a worship service in the Old Testament, and Scripture gives many instructions on how it was to be performed. The singers and their leaders were to reflect what was taught in the Word rather than emphasize their own feelings and reactions to divinity. How do churches today measure up to this standard?

3. Jerusalem was to be highly regarded and strengthened in the people's regard for it. God had chosen that city, so it was to be treated as holy. Why is this so? What role will this city play when the Lord returns?

4. The wall was dedicated precisely as God indicated. This involved the use of priests, Levites, singers, choirs, and "songs of thanksgiving." The dedication service involved a liturgical use of two processions that marched around the walls of Jerusalem. How important was all of this?

5. Nehemiah returned from his administrative post in the Persian government to lead the necessary reforms in marriage practices, the holy use of Temple property, the people's tithes for the Levites' daily livelihood, and the sacred use of the Sabbath. Is this a principle for us?

Questions for Discussion or Reflection

1. Why was it important to put the singers who were responsible for the service in the house of God "under the king's orders" (11:23)? Why do many pastors today abdicate any role in the manner, content, or style in the worship team's actions or selections of songs, which can take charge of half or more of some services?

2. How important is it to train future leaders in the congregation by mentoring them for those days when the teaching pastor must leave to answer a new call or steps aside from the ministry for other reasons?

3. How important is ceremony in the life of the congregation? When has the congregation gone too far in some of its practices, and when has it not observed enough ceremony to be compliant with Scripture?

4. How must present-day believers carry out the command to "rest" on one day of seven? Should the observance of a Sunday Lord's Day carry any weight for modern believers?

Messianic Jewish
Publishers & Resources

*We are a
three-fold ministry,
reaching Jewish people
with the message of Messiah,
teaching our non-Jewish
spiritual family about
their Jewish roots,
and strengthening
congregations with
excellent resources.*

Over 100 Messianic Jewish
Books, Bibles &
Commentaries available at
your favorite Bookstore.

Endorsed by
Christian Leaders
and Theologians:

Dr. Jack Hayford
Dr. Walter C. Kaiser, Jr.
Dr. Marvin Wilson
Ken Taylor
Stephen Strang
Dr. R.C. Sproul
Coach Bill McCartney
and more!

800-410-7367
www.MessianicJewish.net